BEHIND THE
☆☆☆☆☆☆☆☆☆☆☆☆☆☆☆
RANK

BEHIND THE

☆☆☆☆☆☆☆☆☆☆☆☆☆☆☆☆

RANK

VOL 1

LILA HOLLEY

purposely
created
PUBLISHING

BEHIND THE RANK

Published by Purposely Created Publishing Group™

Copyright © 2017 Lila Holley

Printed in the United States of America

ISBN: 978-1-947054-21-9

DEDICATION

15…1 in 5…20…2.05

This book is dedicated to the 15 percent. At the time this book was written, women made up 15 percent of the United States Armed Forces. This book is written to help the 1 in 5 heal. In 2017, 1 in 5 women Veterans admitted they had been the victim of military sexual trauma. This book is written in tribute to the 20 percent of Iraq and Afghanistan women Veterans who, according to data from the Department of Veterans Affairs (VA), have been diagnosed with post-traumatic stress disorder (PTSD). And to the 2.05, this book is written in your honor. With our words, we honor the 2.05 million women Veterans who selflessly served our nation.

AS YOU READ THESE STORIES, TAKE NOTE

This compilation of courageous, heartfelt stories, painstakingly shared by patriotic women who honorably served our nation, is a must read. It's the classic story of triumph under the direst circumstances. Reading their stories brings to mind the phrase, "Freedom isn't free." I pray that others will become mentally, emotionally, and spiritually free after realizing that they are not alone. I feel honored to read these newsworthy stories. Thanks for your service, ladies; you are true American heroes.

Angela M. Odom
Colonel, Retired
US Army
Author of *BRONCO STRONG: A Memoir of the Last Deployed Personnel Services Battalion*
angelaodom.com

When speaking of phenomenal women, Maya Angelou writes, "Pretty women wonder where my secret lies; I'm not cute or built to suit a fashion model's size." These authors, who decided to divulge their stories, are phenomenal in their own right. These women are sharing their stories for the betterment of others. That is phenomenal! I recommend reading their stories so you can see how truly phenomenal these ladies are.

Makissa Lewis
US Army
Medically Retired

There aren't enough words to describe the courage, inspiration, and transparency of these brave military women who have decided to share some of their sacred stories with the world. *Behind the Rank Volume 1* gives an intimate account of thirty powerful women who are bonded for life by the camouflaged uniform that they proudly wore, and still wear. They seek to be silent no more and give their support to all fellow sisters and brothers in arms who may feel that they are alone in the many transitions we undergo. The world will not only be blessed by the stories shared but also empowered to still achieve greatness after the military.

Venus Agoddess Scott
US Army Veteran
www.inspiringthemassesllc.com

TABLE OF CONTENTS

DUTY TO SERVE

DUTY TO SELF

FOREWORD

It is my distinct privilege and honor to write the foreword for this compilation of very personal short stories as told by these courageous and honest military women, from different backgrounds and experiences, who represent several branches of service. They have each peered deeply into their souls to share with us a very trying moment in their lives—one that captures the essence of who they are. They are fighters, conquerors, overcomers, daring followers, and caring leaders who put on our nation's uniforms and stayed true to their commitment and calling.

As a retired Army Colonel who spent more than twenty-seven years on active duty, I know firsthand the emotions, the issues, the challenges, and the ups and downs they each describe in their stories. Their voices, individually and collectively, must be heard to allow American citizens who did not serve in the military an opportunity to have some knowledge of the personal sacrifices and deep turmoil that those who serve go through, both internally and externally. Internally, women Soldiers often set unrealistic standards for themselves that are not required, and externally, they seek to please those who are "unpleasable."

The military woman's story is unique in as much as there are additional challenges levied upon us just by virtue of being a woman in a "man's profession." Women are equipped to handle and meet the challenges, but there is usually a greater learning curve and a longer assimilation period for us. However, more than anything, my twenty-seven-year Army career taught me that all service members are alike: sometimes fearful of the unknown and of failure, both of themselves and of their team, but determined and dedicated enough to want to give their best in the fulfillment of their service to their battle buddies and our nation.

I salute these ladies for their bravery in telling their story. I encourage you to read their stories and envision yourself, your wife, perhaps your daughter or your granddaughter, your mother or your sister in these circumstances. Feel their struggle, admire their resilience, and applaud their patriotism. Take time to get to know and thank your fellow citizens who have become a part of the enduring legacy of those Americans who are both willing to and do bear arms for the defense of our democratic way of life, our constitution, and our nation.

HOOAH!
Sheila W. Varnado
Colonel, US Army
Retired

INTRODUCTION

Many people consider military women to be extraordinary. But what they do not always consider is that we are extraordinary women who are also dealing with everyday challenges in our careers. Don't get me wrong—we know and understand that *everyone* faces challenges on the job. But when those challenges originate, both externally and internally, that adds a layer of difficulty to the task of resolving such issues. A difficulty unique only to women serving in uniform.

Yes, extraordinary we may be, yet we are much like other women; we're mothers, spouses, sisters, daughters, and friends. The difference is that we have chosen the military as our career choice. And our day-to-day challenges range from intimidation, harassment, discrimination, bullying, poor leadership, and toxic environments, all at the hands of the leaders and battle buddies we must trust with our lives.

Add to that the internal challenges that originate within our minds. Many question how a military woman can just leave her family and children to go off to war. What they fail to consider is the turmoil she endures as she works through the process of leaving behind her family and remaining true to the oath she swore to uphold. We have chosen to serve our country, which means our loyalty lies to both our obligation to serve, something that many of us love to do, and to our families, those we love dearly and have an obligation to protect.

Our internal challenges begin there—the obligation to serve and the obligation to our loved ones. Add to that the internal battle we fight in our minds that we must be ten times better and work ten times harder than our male counterparts, undoubtedly a stressor for most military women, yet a motivator for us to give our all and go above and beyond the call of duty.

Understand that we have duties to fulfill: duty to serve, duty to family, and duty to self. Our hope is that you read our words and take away from these short stories our love of service. We courageously share our stories to bring light to the challenges we face every day as we pursue a career that we love in service of our country. We share our stories to help the generation of women leaders coming behind us in hopes of encouraging them to "hang in there," to speak up when faced with challenges, to hold the system accountable to protect them and to hold their leaders accountable to provide environments where they can thrive as the outstanding leaders they aspire to be.

Join us on this journey of storytelling
as we go behind the rank.

DUTY TO
FAMILY

FAITH, FAMILY, AND FORTITUDE

☆ ☆ ☆ ☆ ☆

ABENI CELESTE SCOTT

Service

My time in the military has been the most honorable experience in my entire life, and it was only enhanced by my ability to provide for my family throughout my career. My family means more to me than any other thing in this world.

I left home for the Army in February of 1997. I was eighteen years old, just eight months out of high school, and I had never lived on my own or been away from my mother or grandparents for an extended period. As the oldest of my mother's five kids, it was tough leaving behind all my babies (siblings). Up until that point, my mother wasn't really a single mother because she had me to care after my three-year-old brother (Little Brother), five-year-old sister (Baby Sister), seven-year-old sister (Little Sister), and my God-sent nine-year-old sister (Little "Big" Sister). Nonetheless, I left with excitement to embark on something so courageous.

While in training, I called home to check on my family. I spoke with my grandfather, who informed me that my mom had been over the night before, crying because I was no longer there. This news changed my mood of excitement and made me sob. *Why did I call home? Had I made the wrong decision to leave my mama and my babies?* I knew I had to shake off the guilt because my goal was to stay and do something positive with my life. I could not go back to Miami and attempt community college; that was not supposed to be my story. The Army was my ticket to travel the world and make a better life for my siblings. They were my motivation and I their role model.

The first two years of my military career were great. I was stationed at Fort Bliss, Texas, had been to Saudi Arabia, and had met my best friend, Rasheeda, who hailed from Jacksonville. To top it off, I was loved by so many in my unit. But at home, life had taken a turn for the worse for my mother and siblings. In April 1999, my mother gave birth to my baby brother. He had traces of cocaine in his blood so Child Protective Services threatened to take him and my sisters from my mother. I informed my unit chain of command and, without hesitation, they contacted a unit at Southern Command in Miami and temporarily attached me there while I tended to my family business. It was comforting to have leadership who understood how important my family was to me. I went home and addressed the many troubling situations my family faced. I can honestly say it was my faith that got us through this period. Once my family was situated, I returned to Fort Bliss to continue on the path set before me.

Commitment

I made a habit of going home to visit my family every six months after joining the Army because it was my responsibility to stay in my mother and siblings' lives; it was my responsibility because they were my babies, right? The Army was my career, but I felt that my primary responsibility was to my family at home. I sometimes felt guilty about leaving them, but I knew this was something I needed to do to make life better for all of us.

Many of my friends couldn't understand my dedication to my family. They often questioned why I stressed and worried myself about kids who weren't mine. But I always stayed true to my beliefs. Leaning on my faith, and with the support of my unit and friends, I knew I had what it took to accomplish my mission as a Soldier and still be there for my family.

In January 2003, I was stationed in Germany. Being overseas was the most difficult time in my career as I was unable to just hop on I-95 and drive to Miami to see my family. Multiple deployments and the lack of cell phone service made this time mentally challenging for me. My mother continued to struggle with her life challenges, and unfortunately, my siblings were caught in the crossfire. When it was time to leave Germany, the situation at home had escalated. I decided that Mama and my siblings would join me at Fort Stewart, Georgia. Having my family with me filled my heart, and knowing that I was doing all I could to provide for them gave me so much peace of mind.

With my family safe in Hinesville, I headed to my third deployment to Iraq, which turned into a fifteen-month tour! So much had happened since the nine years I had joined the Army. My little "big" sister lost her high school sweetheart and daughters' father to a heart attack; my siblings lost their father to cancer, and five weeks before redeployment, I lost my grandfather to cancer. Three important men in my life all lost in a fifteen-month time frame. My command allowed me to return home to attend both my stepfather and my grandfather's funerals even though it was five weeks before redeployment. For that, I was so very thankful.

Legacy

In 2009, my father joined me in Hinesville and it was truly heaven on earth. My family remained in Hinesville while I deployed once again in 2009 and then when I headed to Warrant Officer Candidate school. Upon completion of school, my next duty station would separate me from my family, but

I was at peace because we were all in a good place because of God's grace.

Today, my family's legacy includes my little brother currently serving in the military, my little sister raising her beautiful family, my baby sister with two successful careers, my little "big" sister with a successful career, and my mom and baby brother who are busy with their lives and careers in Hinesville. As for me, I'm a Veteran, a retired US Army Chief Warrant Officer after twenty years of honorable service. I am excited to be embarking on an entrepreneurial journey with my sisters with my online boutique, Dress Up Room by Four Girls.

I am so very proud of all that I have been able to accomplish in my military career while supporting and caring for my family. Throughout it all, I was honest and frank with my chain of command, and they supported me in each situation. My command knew that the safety of my family was important to me. When my family's safety and well-being were jeopardized, my performance was negatively affected, but because my command supported me, I was able to perform at peak levels.

My family has been there for me and has made many sacrifices for me these past twenty years. I am forever grateful. I love my family. It's because of them I am the woman I am today.

For God, country, and family!

THE TRUTH BEHIND MY SMILE

☆ ☆ ☆ ☆ ☆

ANGEL RHODES

I Couldn't Help Him

It was September 2008, and I was a schoolteacher in Houston, Texas. I was also a member of the US Army Reserves, and my reserve unit was called up to deploy as a part of Operation Enduring Freedom. My emotions were all over the place, yet I still managed to smile and put on a brave front.

So many thoughts were going through my mind. Who would take care of my family? How would my children survive? Would my two-year-old remember me in a year? Then there was my husband, who would be left to care for our three children alone. All of our family was back home in South Carolina.

We were deployed to Kuwait. This was considered by most as a relatively "easy" deployment since we weren't actually on the battlefield. As a logistician, I worked at the port to ensure that the Soldiers who were on the battlefield had all their necessary supplies. This was the same job that I held during Desert Storm. While my Desert Storm deployment prepared me for the work, what it could not prepare me for was the heartache, loneliness, sadness, and guilt that I experienced as a result of being away from my family.

During Desert Storm, I was a college student and had no husband or children. Our unit was like a family. Since I am a natural nurturer, I quickly assumed the role of Mama Bear. I thought I was doing a great job of training our younger Soldiers and being a great listener for them while they struggled with handling their first deployment. That was until one young Soldier could no longer deal with being away from his family and took his own life. That was and still is one of the darkest days of my life. The fact that he didn't come to me and that I wasn't able to help him made me feel like a complete failure. The guilt sent me into a deeper and darker depression.

I Couldn't Help Myself

I say deeper and darker because what no one else knew, what I refused to share with anyone, was the fact that the strength and the beautiful smile that everyone always complimented me on were just my ways of masking the hurt and pain of depression that I was experiencing. Behind my smile, I was struggling with depression from being away from my own family. I shared their fears of being ambushed on our thirty-minute commute to and from work. I wouldn't admit to sleeping with and regularly carrying a knife for fear of being sexually assaulted in the middle of the night or while showering.

There was no one I could tell that I cried myself to sleep at night because I missed my family, or that my marriage was strained by the long period of separation. There was no one I could share my secrets with. After all, I was the "Mama Bear." I had to be strong and supportive for everyone else. So I painted on a smile and compartmentalized my feelings and emotions to avoid having to deal with them and, more importantly, to prevent anyone from ever knowing that Mama Bear was struggling and battling depression.

When I returned home, it then became my family's problem. Depression affected my marriage and my children in ways that I never would have imagined. I thought that if we just gave it enough time, things would get better. They didn't. In fact, they grew worse.

Yes, I was back at home with my family, but at the same time, I was so far away. My family had developed a new system of running the house—one that didn't include me. I felt useless, so I withdrew even more. It broke my heart to overhear my children asking, "Daddy, what's wrong with Mommy?" or to have them ask, "Mommy, are you okay?" on the days I struggled to get out of bed.

The Truth Behind My Smile

Eventually, I trained myself to go through the motions while they were at home. I would lie in bed all day and then get up just before everyone returned from work and school to greet them with my painted-on smile. When the sadness lingered on, I finally worked up the courage to visit the VA. The doctors diagnosed me with depressive disorder and suggested that I see a counselor. I scheduled the appointment but never returned. How could I, Mama Bear, possibly have a mental health issue? Whatever this thing was, surely I would eventually shake it off. So again, I smiled my best smile and compartmentalized my feelings and my emotions. This was my way of surviving the depression.

My husband later noticed that I was becoming increasingly distracted and forgetful and having a hard time focusing on things. I simply brushed it off as no big deal. I mentioned these symptoms during my annual physical as I spoke with a mental health counselor. She told me these were signs that I was suffering from post-traumatic stress disorder (PTSD). Once again, I brushed this off because there was no way that Mama Bear could have been that severely affected by the deployment.

I was too fearful and ashamed to openly admit that I had mental health issues; that was the truth. In fact, I had been back home and suffered in silence for years before I finally accepted my reality, walked in my truth, and agreed to get the help that I so desperately needed. I was extremely afraid of the negative stigma often associated with mental illness. I didn't want to be seen as weak, and I had heard the negative comments made behind the backs of Soldiers when others found out that they were struggling with their mental health.

I heard a pastor say, "Just like you would go to see a doctor for problems with your physical health without giving it a second thought, you should also be quick to get help for your mental health." When I finally opened up, I was placed on medication. But medication alone was not enough. I also needed someone to act as my sounding board. Just being able to talk to someone made me feel as though a boulder had been lifted from my shoulders. And now when I smile, it's to share my joy and not just an attempt to mask my pain.

I earnestly encourage any of you who may be struggling with depression to do yourself a favor and seek help sooner rather than later. Please know that you are not alone and that reaching out for help does not make you weak. In fact, it has just the opposite effect. Reaching out for help empowers you to walk in your God-given strength, to operate in power and love, and with a sound mind. Your family deserves it, but more importantly, *you* deserve it!

MY TITLE WAS MY WHY

☆ ☆ ☆ ☆ ☆

DE'MEATRICE 'DEE DEE' HODGES

Motherhood

I was called many different names during my Army career. I was called Soldier, Private, Private First Class, Specialist, Sergeant, and Staff Sergeant. But the one name that I will hold so very dear to my heart forever is *Mom*. No other name changed the very essence of who I was like the title Mom. In that moment of finding out I was to become a mother, the only thing that mattered most was to survive for my child. Life was no longer about my friends or hanging out after work. It was not about buying new clothes and shoes or deciding where I should vacation. Being a mother is about providing the very best life to my child.

I gave birth to my beautiful baby girl in January 2001. She was born at 2 a.m. and weighed seven pounds and five ounces. Many who give birth are surrounded by their family, friends, and husbands. I was not fortunate to experience that, however, though I experienced a difficult pregnancy and delivery, I would not change it for anything in the world. I had not only become a mother but a single mother. My daughter's father and I went our separate ways while I was six months pregnant. I was alone and had to grow up very quickly. I had no one to help me because I was stationed so far from home, and I became exhausted while juggling serving my country and being a mother to my daughter.

Called to Serve

The same year I became a mother was one of the worst times in our country's history. I woke up early on the morning of September 10, 2001, excited to take the journey home to California. I loaded myself and my daughter into our car and headed to the airport. Our day was wonderful. Even though this was my daughter's first time flying, she was quiet and calm. Late that evening, we arrived at my grandmother's home and went to sleep. The next morning, I awakened to many missed calls on my phone and my grandmother in a panic. There, as I stood with my newborn daughter, I watched as the Twin Towers fell. I immediately called in to let my chain of command know that I was all right. September

11, 2001, is a day that forever changed how I view mother-hood and my service to our nation as a Soldier.

When I returned home, the atmosphere was different. I could feel the heartbreak, anger, fear, and tension in the air. Rumors of war began to circle. All I could think about was not wanting to leave my baby girl. Then the day came when all my fears became my reality. I was to deploy to Iraq and go to war. My only thought was, Lord, I love my country and I chose to defend her even if my life depends on it, but I am a mother now. I can't leave my daughter and I don't ever want her to forget me.

How does one leave their child behind to fight a war? I asked myself that question many times. One night while I was in prayer, I asked the question again, and this time, my answer was revealed. God spoke to me in such a sweet and calm voice, saying, "As you do what I called you to do, I will take care of your house." God had called me to serve my country just as I serve Him.

My Will to Fight

I left for deployment some time later with just a picture in my pocket and my daughter in my heart. After a few months of being away from my daughter, I thought I would go crazy. All I could think about was the sound of her voice, and hold-ing her tight. The ten-minute phone calls were simply not enough. I conducted my missions during the day and cried myself to sleep during the night.

On one particular mission, we were delivering some equipment, and an improvised explosive device (IED) went off three trucks behind my vehicle. We were in combat! As we fought, my heart raced and images of my daughter ran through my mind. Something sparked inside of me, and my instincts to fight surfaced. As the gunshots rang in my ears, screams began to follow. It was like watching a movie on television, but this was my reality. We fought for what seemed like forever.

Once the quietness returned, we conducted our accountability and returned to our forward operating base (FOB). That day, something ignited inside of me. No longer was I a mother in the Army; I was a *warrior mom*. My country will always be dear to my heart, but my daughter was my number one why. I refused to allow anyone or anything to stand in my way of going home to my daughter. I fought my way back to her. Lives were lost and others forever changed, but I refused to give up.

The months went by, missions came and went, but my prayers grew stronger. My faith and my daughter's voice resided within me. I quoted Psalm 91 every day. I was so overjoyed when we began to prepare to go home, but as we continued to prepare, anxiety set in. I had been gone for so long, I didn't even know if she would recognize me.

When the day finally came, we lined up in formation in the gym. I was so nervous. All I could think was, *would she recognize me?* As the ceremony went on, so many thoughts raced through my mind. My heart was hurting for my fellow Soldiers who had lost their lives. The images of death and violence crowded my dreams. Then came the words we all longed to hear: "Welcome home. You're dismissed." It took everything in me to hold my composure. There she was standing, with her adorable pigtails. I had missed so much during my time away; she was so big now. Tears streamed down my face as I walked up to her.

With a loud scream, she said "Mommy!" She grabbed my neck and said, "I missed you, Mommy."

Though she was young, she never forgot who I was. And that precious title God gave me to wear forever—Mom—was and still is *my why*.

FAITH DURING THE TRANSITIONS

☆ ☆ ☆ ☆ ☆

FANNY MINNITT

Goal Disrupted

My goal was not to join the Army and "be all that I could be." I joined the Army to travel around the world. My first duty station transitioned my mindset in regard to the Army's core goals. For the first time in my life, I had to immediately focus on a lifestyle that seemed to be an illusion to me.

My first day in Fort Jackson, South Carolina, I had to drop and do one hundred pushups for running my mouth. I quickly learned the Army intended to develop me into a Soldier ready to fight for our country. While serving in the military, my experiences were both challenging and rewarding. I received awards and moved quickly up the ranks. You would think that being a part of an organization that rewarded me would make me happy, but I always felt that something was missing. I believe this is why I found myself doing things that were out of character. Although I trusted in God, my faith constantly wavered while I was in training. I moved on to my first duty station in Germany and was ready for any challenge the Army had for me. But my mental state of mind was forever changed.

I am a Christian, but being single and away from home gave me, in my mind, the right to do whatever I dreamed of doing, so I did whatever entered my mind. I even allowed someone to shave all my hair off my head just because I felt like it. Shaving my head signified that I could do whatever I wanted to do, and I thought I was in complete control over my life. I realized later that I was lost while adjusting to the Army lifestyle. I learned some hard lessons, and I hope that wherever you are that you keep the faith and never allow your environment to dictate your actions.

Now, everything I did was my choice, but later I realized that I had an enemy lurking inside of me. Part of my behavior was because I was successful in the Army, but I wasn't successful in my heart. I was working outside of my passion, but I was not about to leave the military because I was succeeding in a career that was predominately a man's world. I felt tough.

My next duty station was Fort Polk, Louisiana, where I met my husband, who is a wonderful man. I know that God sent him to me. While we were married, the time came for me to reenlist, but I found out that I was pregnant. We knew other couples who chose to have their parents raise their children while they continued their military careers, but we decided it was our responsibility to raise our own child.

After eleven years of being in the Army, I decided to separate from the military to take care of my son. I imagined life after the military would be better, but the transition into civilian life was hard. I immediately realized that I had lost my identity and did not know how to get it back, even with being married to a man who loved me. I soon became his friend-enemy. I also had another enemy lurking within me—envy—due to my desire to continue serving my country, which was something my husband was still able to do. He was doing something that I missed doing after separating from the military. I did not tell my husband or anyone else about how I was feeling. I just decided this was my life.

Goal Realized

This created another transition for me, but I smiled and pretended to be happy. All the while, the enemy lurking within me turned up the heat. I was no longer a part of the team. I missed getting up in the morning before day, shooting guns, driving Jeeps, and leading Soldiers. I felt insignificant. I hated going to the commissary on the military base because I felt like I needed my husband's approval. He never treated me this way, but if I didn't have that military card on me, I could not make a purchase. I would get upset when my husband entered the house with his uniform on after work. This was crazy! For some reason, I was blaming him for how I was feeling. He had no idea. I wondered what he thought of me. I was once a Soldier; now I was this dependent. I even wondered what others thought about me when I pulled out my ID card. I wanted to scream, "I am a Soldier!" when I was out with my husband and he was in uniform. And not only was I a friend-enemy to my husband, but I was also a friend-enemy to every other dependent wife with children I met. I felt like a shadow.

"Now Faith is the substance of things hoped for,
and the evidence of things not seen."

—*Hebrews 11:1 KJV*

I was losing hope—hope in ever being all that I could be. I could no longer identify with who I was, and that was a strange place to be in. If you find yourself in a strange place during transition, feeling things inside that you can't explain, get help. Don't become a friend-enemy to the people you love and the people you meet.

The turning point in my life was when I decided to get back into the Word of God. That was when I realized that I was blessed with a great man, great friends, and a great life. My goal now is to appreciate it all. When I look back at all the transitions in my military life, the only thing that I would do differently is embrace every moment that God allowed me to experience. I am so happy, and it is because I know who I am. I believe all things work for my good. Love your military journey, in uniform and after your career, and embrace your transitions.

STAY FOCUSED ON YOUR WHY

☆ ☆ ☆ ☆ ☆

FATIMA R. WILLIAMS

My Turning Point

"I'm sorry, but we are going to have to let you go."

Those were the words that propelled my life into an unknown direction. However, while it was unknown to me what I was going to do next, my stomach knew what it was going to do—violently convulse as I threw up.

I had such a violent reaction to being let go from my job because I was a single parent staying at my mom's house with no financial assistance. When you become a parent, life does not begin nor end around you; your life becomes about the health and protection of your child. And once I was let go, I had no way of providing even those necessities for my daughter.

For the next week, I left the house as if I was going to work. I spent the day sleeping in my car or parked at random businesses. My mother was very judgmental and I did not believe she would understand my current situation because I was the one who was supposed to "have it all together."

I prayed and I cried as I submitted applications to every place imaginable. I just needed a job. During this time of searching and praying, I ended up applying for a job in a shopping center where the Armed Forces Recruiting Station was located. I sat in the car and contemplated and prayed, "Should I, or shouldn't I?"

Then God whispered to me and said, "In your prayers you said you trust me so TRUST ME."

I unbuckled my seat belt and took the first step that led me to a nine-year Air Force career. Looking back, I cannot imagine my life without my experience of serving in the military. Nothing about the beginning of my Air Force career was great. Leaving my daughter to go to Basic Training was one of the hardest things I had to do. But, as you can imagine, she was my motivation to finish and finish on time. During my time in Basic Training, I was blessed to have a Training Instructor who found out that I was a single parent and he would arrange for me to have to do an "extra duty." No, nothing explicit—he would give me an opportunity to make a five-minute phone call to my daughter on occasion. I will forever be grateful to this man because he knew those phone calls would keep me going, and they did.

Historical Turning Point

I made it! Basic Training was over, and I was finally able to see and hold my baby again. Well, not so fast. On the morning of September 11, 2001, I received a Red Cross message that my grandmother had passed away. Reeling from the news, I tried to get myself together for the morning activities, despite the fact that my internal world had just been rocked.

Then, just a few more hours into the morning, the entire world as we knew it changed forever. There we sat, soon to be the Air Force's newest Airmen, and watched the second plane hit the Twin Towers. We knew the life and peace we had known would forever be changed. Due to the attack, we did not have a graduation from Basic Training because we were locked down and no one was allowed on base. We graduated under the awning of our dorms, and then I got on a bus to Alabama for the funeral of my grandmother and to finally hold my baby in my arms again.

The hardest part about being a single parent in the military was leaving behind my child. While I knew what my "why" was, that very thing that motivated me, my children may never truly understand that most decisions were made based on them. Knowing this, however, did not make it any easier when I had to leave my family after the funeral services to go to Keesler Air Force Base, Mississippi, for training, causing me to be away from my baby for another eight weeks. This time, we got through it a lot easier. My first duty station was at Wright-Patterson Air Force Base in Dayton, Ohio, where I had an amazing support system of friends and supervisors.

Clear About My Why

In my career, I would go away for school, training, and deployment, always leaving my daughter for the service of my country and her welfare. One particular training took place on base, where I regularly reported for work at about three o'clock in the morning. Of course, I brought my daughter because there was nowhere for her to go; the daycare was not open at that time.

I will never forget what my OIC (officer in charge) said to me: "If the Air Force wanted you to have a child, they would have issued you one."

While he laughed, I did not. It took everything in me not to respond back with a smart remark, but as always, my thoughts were on my daughter. I couldn't say or do anything to jeopardize my career or our livelihood. Many who have never worn the uniform will not understand the pain it causes a mother to make a career choice that will knowingly take her away from her child, a career that also allows her the ability to provide for her child.

Today, I stand before you a proud Air Force Veteran, forever grateful for the opportunity to serve and grow into a woman of strength. My daughter is proud of the woman I am; she appreciates the sacrifices I had to endure during my military career. While my beginning was not great, I now know it's not where you start that matters most but how you end; and my future is full of unlimited successes!

TRUSTING GOD DURING THE RIDE

☆ ☆ ☆ ☆ ☆

SHANNON CLARK

Roller Coaster Ride

Never did I imagine that in 2016 I would still be in the Army and enjoying it. My career has truly been a roller coaster ride. As a young Soldier, I became so afraid of failing that I never took time to experience the ride. I played it safe and never put myself in positions to fail. I wanted to be like a tree in the middle of the woods—there, but not there. However, God didn't make me to blend in and somehow, I was always selected for special missions and assignments within the organizations I served.

My humbleness, hard work, goofiness, and dedication to making organizations better always got me noticed. In 2011, shortly after delivering twins, I was selected to be a Basic

Leader Course Instructor. At the time, I was certain I could be an Army instructor, but I was uncomfortable with how the position was going to affect my ability to be a wife and a new mother. My body hadn't fully recovered and having a husband that was also in the military heightened my concerns. Every day for three weeks I asked myself how was I going to make it. How was I going to be a good mother while working between nineteen and twenty hours a day? Are my children going to feel my love? Is this assignment going to draw a wedge in my marriage? Am I going to meet the expectation of the organization?

Due to these negative thoughts, I did everything in my power to not be selected as an Army instructor during the training phases. I skipped steps during my evaluation, I was aggressive in receiving feedback, and I maintained a negative presence throughout training, but none of it worked! After my evaluation, I was told that while I performed poorly, I was going to be given another opportunity to teach the block of instruction. This meant I had to stand out in the hall and wait while four other people gave their fifty-minute classes. While I was waiting, a senior instructor walked over to me and told me that he knew what I was doing and it wasn't going to work. I told him all of my concerns, and he told me, "If you are here and they are giving you another chance, it's for a reason."

After he left, I walked into the bathroom that was in the hall and began to cry. I questioned God and why I was in this situation. You see, I'd prayed for years to have children and by that point I'd had two miscarriages. I felt as if God was punishing me for past mistakes.

While sitting in that bathroom, I started talking to myself, and in an effort to pull myself together, the song "It Is for Me" began to play in my head. I walked out of that bathroom with a renewed spirit. I stood in the hall, repeating to myself over and over again, if He brought you to it, He will bring you through it. When it was my turn to reenter the classroom to teach, I did so flawlessly and was selected to be an instructor.

Enjoying the Ride

In that moment, I felt accomplished and I was at peace with my situation, but my personal life still posed challenges in my professional life and, as a newly assigned instructor, having to report to work every Monday through Saturday at 0400 and leave around 1900 to 2000, I was stressed out. My children were enrolled at an in-home childcare center, which provided my husband and me with some flexibility. Not being able to spend time with them was still very much disappointing and caused anxiety, and for the first few months, after dropping my children off at daycare, I would get back in my vehicle and cry the entire way to work.

There were some days when my children didn't see me at all. My husband took them to daycare and picked them up. They were asleep when I got ready for work and when I came home. I suffered in silence; no one knew how I felt, but I got through it. When I pulled into the academy every day, I pulled myself together and put on my Noncommissioned Officer hat, hiding who I was and what I was truly feeling.

Over time, I established myself as an instructor and realized my children weren't affected in any way. The twins knew me and to this day, with all of the moving around that we have done, my marriage is strong and I can't keep my children off of me. During the assignment, I actually had time to have another baby and complete a bachelor's degree. My children appreciate me and are very proud of what I do. This single assignment was the highlight of my career and presented other opportunities to instruct and mentor thousands of Soldiers, both commissioned and noncommissioned.

What I thought was going to destroy me, established me. I was able to gain a holistic view of the Army and write and correct lesson plans. My marriage was strengthened because of this assignment because we had to truly work as a team, and as I watched him support me and push me, love was given a new meaning for me. This assignment revealed who I am, what I am capable of, and what a great man God put into my life to support me along my journey. You see, when you sit on a roller coaster in fear of the experience, you miss the joy of feeling the wind, seeing the amusement park from a different angle, and laughing at the person seated next to you. I believe God has a plan for all of us, but how can the plan be fulfilled if we are too afraid to get on the ride?

A MOMMY'S MILITARY JOURNEY

☆ ☆ ☆ ☆ ☆

SHARON FINNEY

Desire to Serve

I am the daughter of a stay-at-home mom and military dad. Though my parental journey was different, I admire my mother's choice. After high school, I attended college and joined the Army as an officer. I soon learned that I was expecting my first child, so I made plans to leave the military. It wasn't a perfect plan by any stretch of the imagination, but I knew I wouldn't do well actively serving and parenting, or so I thought.

Three years and two children later, I was a civilian wife, mother, and kindergarten teacher. I often struggled with trying not to think like a Soldier and questioned my decision to leave the military, even though I knew I wanted to be a mother who would be available for her kids. Would it have been worth it to just stick it out?

When my youngest was fifteen months old, I separated from my kids' father and prepared for life as a single parent. I didn't know how it would work, but I knew in my heart that this was in our best interest. The divorce process lasted an entire year and even required a special hearing for change of domicile (to relocate to another state). I desperately sought options to insure consistent provisions for my children. I researched the possibility of returning to the military and figured the reserve component would be best.

Being a full-time ROTC contractor while serving in the Reserves mirrored being active duty without some of the demands. This seemed safe enough for my circumstances, so I applied and was selected and restored to the rank of Captain. I began to feel whole again. In August of 2001, I celebrated a year back in uniform and considered growth opportunities. I had returned to the military at what seemed like a peaceful time. But a month later, America faced a major crisis like none other: 9/11. In total disbelief, a coworker and I watched on a small office television as a plane hit the Twin Towers.

In the three hours or so that elapsed from first hearing of the Twin Towers to my departure from work, my mind became filled with scattered thoughts. I drove across town in a fog. I picked my children up early from school, went home, and watched one news report after another. We later attended church to pray with family, friends, and community members. While at the altar, my spirit knew we were going to war. Having deployed before, I knew the Reserve component could easily be activated if necessary. *Lord, You know why I came back to the military*, I prayed. *I wanted to provide for my children without requiring anyone's help. Why is this happening? I know what I signed up for, but I don't want to leave my children.*

Hard Decision

After 9/11, I became a single mom who had three kids and was preparing for deployment. By the grace of God, I secured arrangements and my children quickly settled into their temporary home. They had the love and support of aunts, uncles, godparents, grandparents, and family friends. I left my minivan and more clothes and toys than three kids could ever use. But in the hustle and bustle, I experienced stress on another level. I gained twenty pounds in less than two months—not from unhealthy eating, but just from being overwhelmed. I thought I was handling my affairs well, but another story was unfolding.

Stress, depression, and frustration are a few of the symptoms I experienced in the months leading up to and after that deployment, which was very different from my Desert Storm days. I did my job effectively and efficiently, but when duty hours ended, I was forced to face my internal pain and anguish. I wish I could erase how I masked the pain, but I guess it is all a part of my story.

I requested leave at the four-month point because I desperately wanted to see my precious angels. They showed up at the airport expecting to pick up a family friend but learned it was Mommy. My voice cracked as I called out to them. I grabbed my daughter and fell to the floor as the boys rushed toward us for a group hug.

Within hours of being stateside, I knew their routine and was able to plan our week. I grinned constantly, observing the obvious changes in their smiles and voices. The next day, I visited their school. I wanted to see and do it all! But my heart was broken when my baby girl's teacher said, "We have never seen how beautiful her smile is until now."

Deployed-mommy guilt took over, as our time together began ticking away. *I just got here*, I thought. I already had to prepare to go back. In my mind I wondered, *why did I do this to us?*

When our reunion ended, we had lunch together at the airport. Nothing could prepare me for the coming moments. As my sons stood side by side saying, "Bye, Mommy," I felt so proud. But then I noticed my baby girl in her uncle's arms, with her head on his left shoulder. She would not look my direction, nor would she say a word. If my brother said anything, it was a blur because I was just as sad as my devastated child. By this point, my heart felt like it had broken into a million pieces. The cracking of my voice returned, but this time it was out of pain, not joy. I kept saying, "I love you guys.

I'll be back soon." I didn't know when I'd be back, but it was the thing to say.

Tears poured from my eyes as somebody guided me to my seat on the plane. Blinded by tears and overcome with sadness, I confirmed in-flight the need to hang up my boots for good. Admittedly, it was nice to wear my rank and, of course, I felt a complete sense of pride being able to provide for my children the way I wanted to, but I knew another activation of my unit would be unbearable. There was no way I could leave again. I needed the Lord to make another way for us.

I returned from the deployment six weeks later, just in time to spend Thanksgiving with my family. By January, my paperwork was submitted to become an inactive reservist. I had no service obligation, so this process went a lot smoother than anticipated. I remained inactive for another year and then received my honorable discharge from the US Army. By that time, I was established in a civilian assignment with a comparable salary.

Without judgment, I salute my military sisters who are moms dealing with deployments. Some remain by choice while others are there feeling there are no other options. For me, staying seemed impossible. I did what I could for as long as I could. I am in a different place now, and much to my surprise, all three of my precious angels know firsthand what it means to "support and defend."

HE GOT AWAY

☆ ☆ ☆ ☆ ☆

TAMARA PURNELL

Four Years Wait

The day I had been waiting for had finally arrived. I was on my way from Baltimore to a small town in Pennsylvania to get my beautiful baby girl tested for paternity. It had been a long hard struggle to get to that point. The laws are so different in every state, but in order for my daughter's father's name to be on her birth certificate without us being married, he had to sign an affidavit, which he refused to do and which brought me to this point. It took four years to get him to take the paternity test.

Being in the military had made things a little difficult. My daughter was conceived in 1984 in Jacksonville, North Carolina. Then in 1985, I received orders to Yokosuka, Japan, and in 1988, I headed to San Diego, California. The timing was finally perfect to get this done. I was on leave, so we could be tested before I left for the West Coast.

As fate would have it, we ran into road construction, which made us late for our scheduled appointment. When I walked into the hospital lobby, a nurse met me and stated, "We've been waiting for you. The young man was here, but he left."

I called my daughter's father and asked if he was coming back, and he informed me that he wouldn't be back. I then informed the nurse that the young man wouldn't be returning and we would proceed with the test without him. After we were tested, we drove back to Baltimore and I flew to San Diego the next day. Because I was going to be stationed onboard a ship, I left my daughter in Baltimore with my family.

The ship was preparing for a Western Pacific (West Pac) tour, and we would be at sea for at least six months. This was my first time being separated from my only child and my first time on a ship. I went with an open mind but was full of expectations. Life was good. I was learning my job (rate) and getting used to life on the ship. When I was asked how I liked being on a ship, my reply was that it was no different than working in an office. It just so happened that my office was located on a ship.

The day arrived when we were pulling out for sea. I was getting a little antsy waiting for the DNA results. I had waited for three years, so a few more months couldn't hurt, right?

Wrong. I will never forget the day when the letter arrived. I was on the signal bridge with a very close friend of mine, excited about finally receiving the results. *This* was the proof that I had been waiting for. I opened the letter, and tears began to run down my face. The letter read that it was *impossible* for him to be her father. *This was a lie.* That bastard had gotten away! I was so angry and upset. My friend just held me while I cried.

I Knew the Truth

I knew who my child's father was and *he knew* he was her father. I wondered, did he hate me that much that he would have someone else take the test? Was he that fearful of the white world he lived in that he would deny his biracial baby? That had to be the answer. It was okay for us to live our lives as a couple in the military, but beyond those walls of protection, he wouldn't let anyone know about us.

He surely wouldn't let his friends know. How could he laugh at those nasty racial jokes that they told amongst each other? The most hurtful part of it all was that this man had been my best friend. We were in a loving relationship. We had spoken about marriage; he was not some one-night stand. Everything was good, or so I thought. I was crushed because I couldn't run and hide. I had another person to think about—our daughter—whom I would raise even if I had to raise her alone.

Even though I was disappointed, I realized that at the end of the day, my daughter was my responsibility. Had her father still been in the military, I could have gone to his unit commander and he would have been made to pay child support. However, he was now a civilian, and I had no other recourse. Hell, I had been taking care of her for the last three years by myself anyway! And I would continue to take care of her for the rest of her life, as needed. I had a strong family support system, so I knew we would be fine. However, it seemed to me that he had gotten away, yet again, from the responsibility of caring for our daughter. The strangest thing is that even to this day he has never denied that he is her father. He just has never wanted the responsibility of being a father. At least not to our child.

I share a piece of my story because I'm sure there are young women out there who are in similar situations. I share it because as women and mothers, we are lions when it comes to our children. I worked three jobs to ensure my daughter had everything that she needed. Would her life have been any better with the love of a father? Probably, at least emotionally anyway. For a very long time, I couldn't understand how a man could turn his back on his own flesh and blood. Life has made me understand that fear will make people run and hide. Running and hiding was not an option for me. I had to work with the hand that life dealt me; we all must. I wouldn't trade my journey for anything or anyone else's. We made it! And we are better for it. My daughter is a very caring, funny, lovable young lady who has blessed me with three beautiful grandchildren.

ARE YOU TRUE TO YOUR "I DO"?

☆ ☆ ☆ ☆ ☆

TAREKA ROBINSON

Do You Have Faith in Your "I Do"?

I was fresh out of college when I said "I do." Bright-eyed and in love, I was happy to take my vows before God and family. My new husband was also young, bright-eyed, and in love—in love with the idea of protecting our freedoms in service to our country as a Soldier in the military. He also said "I do" to God and country.

I don't think either one of us had any idea how much our lives would change as a result of us saying those two small words. All we knew was that we were in love. And within twenty-four hours, he was off doing what he loved, off to war to serve our country in a foreign land. I immediately asked myself, *what have I done? What have I really said "I do" to?*

Like many new wives, I questioned if I was ready for all of it. Was I really ready to be married to the military? Then I received the news: I was pregnant.

On that day, I made a decision: I do, I did, and I would remain true to my vows for love of my husband and for love of country. I knew he was dedicated to the vows he took. He could not walk out on his obligation to our country, and I knew I could not walk out on our marriage. He had to leave to fight for our freedom, and I had to leave the comfort of my family and friends to fight to save our marriage.

If my military husband was going to stick to his oath, I would stick to my vows. I do and I did through four deployments, two pregnancies without him, and too many long stretches of separation. Many military wives find themselves in similar situations with tough decisions to make. Do you have faith in your "I do"?

I knew I couldn't let my spouse down just like he couldn't let his guys down. While deployed, he was watching their six, and I was at home watching our six. My actions at home allowed him to focus while in combat, so he was then able to help his guys focus so that they all came back home safely.

Where Is Your Loyalty to Your "I Do"?

Then the day came for my husband to return home. It was time for him to fulfill his obligation to his other "I do": me. I knew my spouse was not going to be the same person he was before he had left, and together, we had to deal with the mental anguish brought on by combat. My husband came home operating at a hypervigilant level; he was always *on*—protective and defensive. He had changed; things had changed. Was I *still* sure about my "I do"?

I had to think things over, and I found myself reflecting back to the lessons I was taught growing up. I grew up in the church—I always went to church—and I had no other choice but to go to church. Somewhere along my journey, I drifted away from the lessons I was taught in the church or by my parents and grandparents. When my husband came home, I knew I could not tackle our challenges by myself. I had to go back to the Word, what I had been taught so many years ago. It took over a year for me to grow in my relationship with God and understand what I was reading in the Word and for it to help me with the situation of my "I do."

Once again, I knew that many military spouses found themselves in similar situations and wondered, *where is my loyalty?* I decided I would do whatever it took to keep my marriage. Yes, it got hard with the children, financial obligations, errors with his military pay, and mental and physical separation from him, but I was loyal. Despite all the trials, I knew it could be a lot worse.

These were the times I really leaned on the Word of God for strength. I recalled a scripture about speaking those things that do not exist as though they were, so I started to speak into my life, my marriage, and our overall situation. I began to see things turn around. I learned that with faith, anything is possible. I had to remain loyal to our vows to learn this lesson. All I needed was faith the size of a mustard seed to make it through and at times that's all I had: a mustard seed–size faith. But it was that faith that helped me turn my "I do" into I can, I will, I shall, and I have.

As my husband watched me make the effort, he knew it was God working on me and through me to change our situation. I felt that if it didn't kill me, why not just do the work and get it done? Taking this attitude made life so much easier. I was not only the wife and mother but the mechanic, yard keeper, electrician, plumber—the list goes on. When I say I did whatever it took to have peace in my home and for my Soldier to be stress free, I did whatever I had to do. Yes, being a military wife is not easy, but it was worth every life experience I had. Would I do it again? Yes, absolutely!

We both stayed true to the vows we took because we believed in faith, truth, and loyalty. We knew if we had *faith* in God, stood in our *truth* during the challenges, and remained *loyal* to our vows, then God had us.

DUTY TO
SERVE

AN APPROVED LEADERSHIP MODEL

☆ ☆ ☆ ☆ ☆

ASHLEY M. BOOKER

Selfless Leader

"Be all that you can be." I stamped that slogan on my heart when I made the decision to enlist in the US Army. As a female Soldier, I prepared myself to keep my head up, my eyes open, and my heart focused on what I aimed to be once I finished training. I aspired to become a great representation of the Army values.

As a leader in the military, I stood strong for justice, fairness, standards, and respect. I strived to be the best and nothing less, and I expected the same from my Soldiers and all those I encountered. I always put the mission first to the point where I grew anxious every moment that I was away from the ranks for any reason other than what the mission required. I made myself sick confirming that all areas were covered, even when others couldn't care less about the next steps needed to accomplish the mission.

I was challenged and provoked, required to prove that I was good enough to keep my position while others were allowed to perform at substandard levels. I buried my problems deeper and deeper, not saying a word because I was needed and my absence would cause the mission to fail—or so I thought. This type of thinking caused me to suffer. I do not wish any service member to suffer; instead, I leave you with a few tips in hopes of helping you dig deep to become a great representation of the branch of service that you serve.

Character

It is commonly stated that communication is key in any relationship. In order to be a great battle buddy, Soldier, and leader, you must effectively learn how to speak to others. When engaged in conversation, if something is wrong, offer a solution. If something doesn't sit well with you, take steps to make changes for the greater good of all. When you are a part of the solution, you can eliminate many problems.

I encourage you to keep an open mind about those you encounter on a daily basis. Your communication with each individual may differ, so here are three important conditions to always consider:

1. Speak to others as you would like to be spoken to.

2. Be discreet and considerate to all elements of the individual before going into conversation with anyone. Apply the five Ws—who, what, when, where, and why—to all situations and scenarios you face. It could change the outcome of the conversation when you get to the root of things.

3. Listen with a fair mind to obtain a justified outcome and solution in all situations.

Personal Life

Get your life together! If you have something in your life that you need to sort out, address it. Take time to resolve it so that it does not obstruct you from being the great leader that you strive to be. Do not allow life's issues to prevent you from putting anything less than your best foot forward. Sometimes we have to step away in order to get ahead. Remember, the military needs us at our best, so don't let things like physical pain, family burdens, children's sicknesses, or mental health build up. Unresolved, these things can take away from the best you that you have to give to the military. A good support system helps greatly: they understand, listen, and provide the assistance needed to push on.

Lead from the Front

This new generation of instructing Soldiers to complete tasks in your absence must stop. Instruct, demonstrate, and follow through. A good leader is not going to know everything, but a great leader is not afraid to inquire and seek knowledge from the subject matter experts around them, no matter the rank. You are never too high or low in a position to learn or teach something. I know from experience, if you pretend to know everything, you will lose others' respect faster than if you are just frank with all who are observing you. Inquire from those with the experience. In some cases, "I don't know" may be the best answer you have for your Soldiers or those seeking answers from you.

The greatest lesson I have learned is to set aside my pride if I want to survive. As a leader, I felt nothing would happen unless I was there, and I placed all tasks in front of my own needs. As a female Soldier, I felt like I had to push harder and be stronger than those around me because along my journey I noticed my peers losing their commitment to the calling to serve. As women, we must stand tall in formation and understand that our work will grow our wisdom and our wisdom will earn us the rank. So remember to take care of yourself first. And *never* hold in your emotions or feel like it is wrong to have emotions. It's okay to have emotions. Make sure you have a healthy system of processing the emotions you feel.

In the military, we receive a lot of information and tough missions. But as a leader, find a way to deliver information in segments that can be received by others so that they will be motivated to accomplish the mission. Create a path that does not make you lose heart in what you do. If you can keep your attitude up and continue to do the right thing, you can reach amazing heights. Keep your head up! You are beautiful, you are strong, and you can truly be all that you can be. Take a leap of faith and expand your reach, keeping the standard that has already been set in place. Be the strong, proud female Soldier that you are and never settle for less than the best!

COURAGE IN MY VOICE

☆ ☆ ☆ ☆ ☆

DR. KAREN MAXFIELD LUNKIN

Where Was My Voice?

After less than three months as the Platoon Leader for a fabulous Signal Corps communications team in Camp Casey, Korea, I, with my team, was selected to provide communications support for an infantry unit that was going on a very important field exercise. I was proud of our unit and excited to show what we could do. I felt the pride and comradery as our unit went about its daily preparation for the upcoming exercise. There's nothing like being a part of a group of people operating to accomplish a common goal and being recognized for our accomplishments. I believe there is no better way to build a team.

That morning, my Company Commander called me from our motor pool: "Lieutenant Maxfield, I'd like to see you in my office this afternoon. We need to discuss the upcoming field exercise."

Excited, I rushed off to the Commander's office to get the latest orders and final details for our platoon's upcoming honored position. My Commander was a forward thinker who welcomed me as a young, African American military leader in his company. I trusted him.

"Have a seat, LT," he began. "Listen, I just got a call from the Battalion Commander of the infantry unit you are preparing to support next week. Unfortunately, I need to report some bad news to you. It appears that the Commander of that infantry unit does not want your platoon to support them on the field exercise because their leader is a woman—you." He paused to look directly into my eyes, "Are you okay with that? Can you handle that?"

He was professional and too mission-focused to spend too much more time asking me about my feelings, but frankly, I did not want to spend any more time than needed discussing the situation. Mainly, I did not want to become emotional in front of my Commander.

Inside, I was crushed, embarrassed, and disappointed for my unit, who was still preparing as we spoke. I was a young, twenty-two-year-old platoon leader, and I struggled to articulate what I was feeling at that time. *Where was my voice?* I felt so inadequate, numb, and defeated, but I needed to speak out. I knew that I needed to stand up. I knew that I needed to speak up, but I was overwhelmed, so I shrunk.

That is one of the experiences I refer to when I am mentoring others, teaching at the university, or just talking with my adult children about taking a stand in their lives. Now, I am so passionate about many things in life that I do not hesitate to take that stand for the things I believe in. I am always enlightened by the power of self-reflection, looking back at my actions and the thought processes that preceded them. I still live with the regret of not finding the courage to raise my voice and speak up in that situation. That was in 1985.

I must be clear that my faith in Jesus Christ was conceived and deeply nurtured during those two very special years in Korea. I memorized Romans 8:28 and saw it come to life through my experiences there. Truly, all things do work together for the good of those who love God and are called according to His purpose, and I know that each of these unique experiences worked together for my good.

Many minority women serving in the military have been in situations where they did not take a stand for themselves or others and later regretted it. The regret could have surfaced years later, as was my case. I regret not taking a stand in the face of blatant discrimination; it has been a heavy burden to carry and I have been extra vigilant because of it.

I was told, "You're too confident for a Lieutenant. You're too cocky to be just a 2nd Lieutenant! I don't like blacks, I don't like females, and I don't like 2nd Lieutenants."

Those words were delivered by my company's First Sergeant, and they stung like the heat from an unsuspected hornet's sting. He was the highest-ranking Noncommissioned Officer in our company, and I really wanted his respect. I must admit that I was stunned by his words. So I did what I always did to hide the disappointment, frustration, anger, and pain: I responded with a hint of humor.

"So I'm guessing you don't like me either?" I quipped.

I have regretted my humorous response all these years later. If I had the opportunity to talk to my younger self, I would tell her that it is not worth the lifelong regret to shy away from confrontation. I would tell her to take a stand now, even if you don't have the vocabulary, knowledge, or support that you feel like you need to face that situation. In hindsight, I would have liked to have been more prepared for situations that arose that literally cut to the core of who I am as a black, Christian woman.

I believe that women are conditioned from an early age to conform, to never disagree—especially with males. In the military, the unspoken rule is that becoming emotional in the face of such situations is weak. My message to young, minority women now and in the future is the same: take a stand, speak your mind, voice your opinion, and call out those people or groups who try to silence you, regardless of the opposition you may face. Be who you are, and be a voice for those coming behind you. Remaining silent or masking your pain will never suffice. So I write, I speak, I craft poetry, I create, I collaborate, and I self-reflect because my heart needs to be heard and honored—and so does yours. Because all things really do work together for my good! Blessings from my beautiful heart to yours.

DRAWING STRENGTH OUT OF A TOXIC ENVIRONMENT

☆ ☆ ☆ ☆ ☆

KRISTINA EATON

Company Command

I've heard it said that being a Commander is the best assign-ment of your military career. Just two months prior to depart-ing Ft. Lee, Virginia, I received notification that I was board selected for company command. I felt excited, nervous, and scared all at once. I was the new incoming Company Com-mander for a transportation company in Southern Alabama. What a privilege and honor. I was up for the challenge, how-ever, I didn't feel quite ready. My faith and optimism carried me through naturally from day to day. However, nothing could have prepared me for what I would experience during my command time. What was supposed to be a very rewarding time in my life turned out to be the most dreadful, exhausting, toxic months in the uniform. That notion, that being a Commander is the best assignment of your military career, is true for some, but it was not for me.

I reported mid-June to my unit and, soon after, we had a new incoming Battalion Commander (BC). The battalion change of command—saying good-bye to our outgoing Battalion Commander and welcoming our new Commander—was a bittersweet moment for me. I really didn't know what to expect. As I stood in front of my platoon in formation, I had a proud moment. I realized that being the only African American female Commander in the battalion was such an accomplishment.

Throughout my career, I did not have many female mentors. My attempts at seeking mentorship from another female officer were often received with resistance, as if providing mentorship would have been a bother to them. It would have been nice to have that mentorship relationship to reference in preparation for this moment. Regardless, I was still very proud and thankful for the opportunity to lead as Commander and was determined to do my best. I knew what a Commander's role was, but secretly, I was anxious going into the position. I knew I would need to lean on my faith more than ever.

Shortly after his arrival, I received a negative counseling statement from my BC. There was no substance to the claims on the counseling statement. I concluded it was a plot to move me out of my position as Commander. I felt ambushed, like I was being attacked. I immediately became defensive, lost trust in everyone, and became paranoid. I created an emotional wall. That was my way of coping.

I was ready to get out of the situation, and I hadn't even completed my first full year as Commander. I contacted the Human Resources Command (HRC) about a reassignment and they said, "Not yet, you haven't even received your first evaluation." So I waited. This was a tough time for me. I had adopted a serious attitude, which in hindsight really didn't help the tense situation with my leadership. But it was hard not to have an attitude when I didn't even like going to work.

Almost Over

During my second year of command, I was forced to participate in a high-visibility training exercise with my Soldiers and equipment, even though my unit was in recovery following a deployment and the mission requirement didn't call for my unit's truck capacity. The battalion staff, as well as my supervisor, knew I was against participating and knew all my reasons why, yet no one seemed to understand nor care. Unfortunately, my Soldiers were involved in a terrible accident, during which they experienced trauma and lost all morale.

Then my BC threatened me with a financial statement for loss of unit equipment (FLIPL). In theory, a FLIPL could have ruined or ended my career. Under no circumstances was that going to happen! I had 100 percent accountability for equipment stored in four states.

Screaming and shouting were commonplace during phone conversations with my leadership. I'm convinced that I was being bullied and intimidated. I was appalled. It was acceptable by everyone around me. I spent months documenting all the events that took place; it kept me so busy that I couldn't really concentrate on being a Commander.

Complaints to the Inspector General Office or the Equal Opportunity Office hit a brick wall. I didn't trust anyone in my chain of command. This was an extremely stressful time for me. I lost a lot of weight during my time in command, which also drained my energy. I was in my own little bubble because I felt so alone and isolated for various reasons. My nights were filled with terror, and this terror only caused more anxiety, which worsened my PTSD.

God's Grace

Once my change of command was over, I moved down the road to work on the battalion staff. I was the Action Officer responsible for planning the battalion field training exercises. There was no proper handoff and no guidance on what my supervisor expected of me. Needless to say, I remained in the same workspace as the very staff who had been bullying me for the past two years while I was in command. I was screamed at and criticized in front of my peers and colleagues. It was humiliating. I made the decision in that very moment that I was done. I couldn't do it anymore. The senior officers who were supposed to be my mentors and my trusted leadership left me out to dry. My only saving grace was just that: God's grace. It was my faith that kept me through these trials. I acknowledged that I lacked guidance and mentorship from the leaders appointed over me, and I started down the road to peace and moving on in my career.

Things began to turn around for me when I met my husband weeks before my scheduled move. The happiness I felt with him outweighed the craziness of my Command assignment. Nonetheless, I was excited about moving closer to home. By the grace of God, I survived. My faith carried me through it all, and although I was going through hell, I still managed to be an encourager to my Soldiers and others around me. This chapter of my life has forever shaped the woman and military officer I am today.

GIRL GOT A GOMOR

☆ ☆ ☆ ☆ ☆

MICHELE M. SPENCER

"No weapon that is formed against thee shall prosper;
and every tongue that shall rise against thee in
judgment thou shalt condemn."

—Isaiah 54:17 KJV

Straight Up Lies

"WTF!" I gasped, as I fell to my knees and clutched my heart in disbelief. I had just received an extremely harsh punishment—a career-killing reprimand from a General Officer for something I did not do. The 15-6 investigation that occurred five months earlier over an alleged claim that I had coerced junior ranking Soldiers to purchase my self-published inspirational war memoir, *B.A.G.H.D.A.D. Yoga A Shift in Consciousness: Fear to Love, War to Peace,* was completely ludicrous! From 2012 to 2015, I was the Executive Officer (AGR) for a medical support battalion. I was a good leader, loyal and trustworthy, and I had earned the respect of our small unit. However, we all know there will always be "haters," those who don't like us for one reason or another. That was the case in my situation. I was straight up lied on! Jealousy, racial contempt, and weak leadership also played into this mockery of a case.

And so, I was on my knees in prayer, in tears, frustrated, angry, demoralized. *I got a GOMOR. Whaaaaaaaaa?* Just one month earlier, I had been selected for promotion to Colonel on my first primary zone look. Earning that rank was a great accomplishment because I had begun my career enlisted and became an ROTC distinguished military graduate and Commissioned Officer. I had always taken the hard leadership jobs when available and remained active in many community service endeavors by voluntarily teaching yoga where I was assigned, from Baghdad, Iraq, to Sacramento, California. I shared the important gift of yoga to promote health and happiness, which is the premise of my aforementioned book.

So that frightful day late in October 2014, with Halloween decorations in full display, I thought it was an evil trick and that I was getting punked. The call came in from my Brigade Commander informing me of the 15-6 investigation final determination from our higher command to file a General Officer Memorandum of Reprimand (GOMOR) in my permanent personnel record. Really? I knew of Soldiers of all ranks—with multiple DUIs, verified sexual harassment complaints, failed drug tests, and overall incompetencies—who were just slapped on the wrist or given counseling statements as punishment.

A mild punishment wasn't an option for me. Instead I would get the complete "beast" beat down over a falsehood. In my book, I describe "a beast is any person, place, or thing that tries to hold you back and deter you from your true self and your purpose in life. Beasts are shadows trying to block your light. Beasts are everywhere…What we do, how we control them or even feed them is entirely up to us. Being an agent of change takes great courage and commitment. It is the ultimate beast changer."

After thirty years of exemplary service with no previous poor performance or bad behavior counseling, this girl got a GOMOR "beast." I was dumbstruck from being singled out unfairly, What would I do?

I'll tell you what—I wiped my tears and got my ass off the floor with the prayer, "No weapon shall prosper." I called my momma to help me pull my shit together! And within the next twenty-four hours, Halloween brought me a "treat": a highly qualified Judge Advocate General Officer (JAG) who would assist me for nearly two years with formal appeals, rebuttals, an EO/IG military congressional complaint, and a case with the Department of Army Suitability Evaluation Board (DASEB). During the last four months of 2016, I also retained a civilian lawyer and private investigator, with whom I took a polygraph test to prove my innocence and bolster my overall case.

I also had to get smart on GOMORs. Besides reviewing Army regulations (AR), I found an excellent layman's article entitled "REPRIMANDS: THE ARMY'S DIRTY LITTLE SECRET" by attorney Lee Stockdale. In short, he asserts that:

> The dirty secret: a GOMOR is the Army's way of punishing Soldiers when the evidence isn't there. The Army requires no standard of proof. AR 600-37, "Unfavorable Information," requires only an "objective decision by competent authority." A General Officer can determine, unilaterally and without external review, that the reprimand be filed in a Soldier's permanent records . . . . The weakness of evidence supporting administrative reprimands is often tragic. Investigations are routinely biased ab initio.

In September 2016, I received notice that by unanimous vote the DASEB granted full relief and determined the evidence presented clearly and convincingly that the GOMOR was untrue and unjust and that it would be removed from my record with promotion reconsideration. *Amen!*

But wait, there's more! At the time of the submission of this story in January 2017, my file was still awaiting adjudication at the Army Board for Correction of Military Records (ABCMR) to reinstate my promotion to Colonel. I share my journey in hopes of encouraging someone to continue to fight the good fight!

Setback to Success

There are challenges, hurdles, obstacles, and beasts that any one of us may face in our personal and professional lives at any time. No one is spared of this human plight. We know full well that we will face betrayal, criticism, humiliation, doubt, frustration, stigmatization, and more, but it is ultimately how we respond to experiences that determine actual success in any setback. Dr. Martin Luther King Jr. said it best: "The ultimate measure of a man is not where he stands in moments of comfort and convenience, but where he stands at times of challenge and controversy."

What is behind the rank? GRACE! **G**od **R**estores **A**cceptance, **C**ourage, **E**mpathy. I continue to serve my nation proudly, knowing that it is imperative to share our stories with no fear. If we see something, we must *say something*.

I will not be a "beast" beat down statistic, nor can you; together, we cannot! Yes, it is painful to be wrongly accused and not have the due process or support necessary to push back. I know of Soldiers who acquiesced to their punishments and were discharged or bitterly decided to retire. It is shameful to watch others get ahead while being morally corrupt, and the innocent have no recourse to fight the good fight for themselves. Not on my watch—we cannot go down like bruised chumps. It takes steely determination and perseverance, so show up, serve, share, and shine!

IT'S NOT TOO LATE

☆ ☆ ☆ ☆ ☆

MICHELE PATTON JOHNSON

"My favorite age is NOW."

—*Kirsten Dunst*

A Shift Takes Place

I arrived at the funeral of a young lady I had worked with at the community recreation center. As I walked to my seat, I heard a voice down in my gut say, "You've outgrown this place." I knew it was God shifting my life, but I never thought it would shift the way it did. My process of elimination started from that day forth. After the dust settled and after a sixteen-year break in service as an active-duty US Air Force Sergeant, I joined the US Army.

I walked into the recruiting center with a mission in mind to get information about rejoining the Air Force. At the time, they were not taking anyone with prior service, but the Air Force recruiter encouraged me to go down the hall and check with the Army recruiting office. Joining the Army was not one of my options so I left. Two weeks later, I was back. There are times in life when God will upset your plan and take you on a journey that is made just for you; this was the beginning of a new journey.

At the time I entered the Army recruiting office, I was forty-one years old. Yes, I know if I had stayed in the Air Force, I would have been retired by that time and probably working on a second retirement. But here I was, ready to take on this new stage in my life. I sat down and talked to the recruiter. He looked surprised when I told him my age, and I became the "guess her age" carnival act in the recruiting station. I didn't have time to waste. I needed to know what I had to do to be a part of the Army.

I completed all the paperwork, and my recruiter told me that I would have to take the over-forty physical. If I could get physically cleared, I was a go for signing up. Well, I had no worries about my physical, so I was ready to process as quickly as possible. Remember, I didn't have much time to spare. I was forty-one years old. I felt like all the recruiters were betting that I wouldn't pass the physical because of my age, but they lost that bet because I passed with flying colors. There was one catch: I had to wait six months before entering because of a prior surgery. But at that time, I realized that age does not dictate the doors that God has opened for you. It's never too late.

Against the Odds

I took the next six months and worked out like an Olympian prospect. I looked up the physical fitness standards for my age and they all seemed doable. So I got on the floor to do the pushups and lo and behold, I could do one whole pushup. I said to myself, "Jesus, be a pushup!" My work was cut out for me, but I would not be beat by my own mind or body. If you have ever started a workout plan or any endeavor in life that seemed hard, you know that you have to be focused on the goal, the return, and the results.

Every day, without fail, I was in the gym, at the outside track, and in my living room, telling my body to do pushups and sit-ups and run. Some days, I felt my body trying to take over the race, and I entered a warzone that I was determined to be the victor in. I was determined that my goal to be physically prepared for the Army would not be beat by my own body trying to give up. Determine that your goal will not be beat by obstacles.

I made it to Basic Training and everything seemed the same: hurry up and wait. But the big difference was this was twenty-four years after going through Air Force Basic Training. It was February 2008 and it was cold and frigid in my departure city of Chicago as well as in my final destination of Fort Sill, Oklahoma. I don't like cold. I have never liked cold. I never will like cold. I thought this would present an obstacle for me. I was older, so my body didn't just snap back as quickly as it used to. There were times when my mind and body went into that warzone and I felt like giving up.

These were the times when I had to go back and draw strength from the words of the Lord that said, "You've out-grown this place." When you have outgrown a place, it can feel like putting on clothes that are too small. Like when we gain a few pounds and try to put those size eight pants on, but we are really a size ten. We have to leave the button of the pants open and wear a long shirt to cover our waistband and extra pounds. It's so uncomfortable and you can't make yourself fit into the space anymore. I had moved out of that uncomfortable space but not without meeting challenges. Challenges make you stronger.

If we are following behind God as we take any journey, we can rest assured that when we get to the destination, He is already there. There is no age limitation on obedience and what God chooses for us to do. We just have to obey. If you have heard God telling you to forward march into a new place and you are still sitting in those old uncomfortable pair of pants, it's time to get up and move. It's time to get in align-ment with the life that God has created for you. If He says go, it's not too late. When you come up against obstacles, don't let them beat you. As you challenge your situations and they challenge you, allow the challenges to make you stronger.

GOD'S GRACE OUTWEIGHS THE SACRIFICE

☆ ☆ ☆ ☆ ☆

NIKEISHA JOHNSON

The most difficult contribution to serving is not
the service itself but rather the SACRIFICE!

Far Greater Sacrifice

Like many Soldiers, I faced difficult challenges in my career.
Challenges that initially made me question every ability I
knew God had placed within me. I've been called to serve
and sacrifice in ways that made me question the reason why
God would allow me to enter into such a career. Everything I
had once believed about myself became distant memories—
memories of self-awareness and confidence, and being filled
with the faith in knowing the best was ahead of me. Joy and

peace were replaced with inadequacy, shame, hurt, anger, hopelessness, and depression. I was eager to serve and to be a part of something greater than myself. I just thought, this must all be a part of the sacrifice.

The sacrifice I speak of was far greater than the racism or sexism I experienced. Far greater than the sexual harassment that was swept under the rug. This sacrifice was even greater than the bullying and disrespect I experienced.

The sacrifice I speak of led me to a very dark place for quite some time, and it was there I realized that my sacrifice had become far greater than my service. The big sacrifice I speak of was a miscarriage, which stole the gift of parenthood from my husband and me.

One in every five women in the military experience miscarriages for various reasons, and I was a part of that pool. I will admit that I had a willful addiction to prove that I belonged in the position that I held at the time. As a female in the military, I felt that I had to always work two times harder than the average male. When compared to the average Caucasian man or Caucasian woman, as an educated African American woman, I felt I had to work ten times harder. The level of stress I experienced greatly impacted my body and led to the miscarriage. Then add to that the depression from losing the baby and the stress caused by people who had no conscience. Can you imagine how it felt to hear leaders in my command say, "It wasn't even a baby yet; it was just a miscarriage"? At that point, I felt like less than a woman. After all I had given the Army, I felt it had taken something from me. The one thing that many women long for is the gift of motherhood. At that point, I felt the sacrifice far outweighed my duty to serve.

Far Greater Grace

Prior to the miscarriage, I was presented with an opportunity to transition to a greater position that would benefit me as a leader. However, I had been encountering racism, sexism, and harassment prior to the pregnancy, and once people knew I was pregnant, the negative and toxic behavior intensified. My command had the simple task of completing the required packet; all that was needed was a signature on one document. But they took actions that were meant to prevent me from gaining the position as well as my promotion to the rank of Captain. I began to panic when I realized my leadership was not going to support me in my career progression.

Then came the excuses. I needed to take another Army physical fitness test (APFT) even though I had recently taken one with the command. Unaware of my pregnancy at the time, I took the APFT. During the run, I noticed I had a severe shortness of breath but thought it was due to the severe stress I had been experiencing. Even after passing the test, I still could not breathe, had severe headaches, and was extremely weak.

My husband said, "You may be pregnant."

I panicked because the first thing I thought was, here's another reason to delay my career progression.

That same day, my pregnancy test read positive. I was so happy, but I knew something did not quite feel right about the pregnancy. I went to the doctor only to find that my stress level was causing severe stress on the baby as well. I kept silent about my pregnancy but sadly, three months later, the doctor ruled that my body was having difficulty trying to dispel the embryo. My heart sank and my first reaction was, *oh my God, look at what I have sacrificed.*

Depression soon filled my world as I endured the process of losing my child. After my body failed to pass (abort) the fetus on its own, I was rushed in for an emergency surgery to complete the process, which was ruled as a spontaneous abortion. The mere thought of the word "abortion" clouded my day, and I cannot begin to describe the pain I felt then and still feel today. What made it worse was the fact that I was in a predominantly male unit, and the insensitivity I received was unbearable. At that point, I felt less than a woman and after all I had given the Army, I felt something had been intentionally taken from me.

Conclusively, experiencing such a unique sacrifice forced me into the arms of God and that's when I truly learned the meaning of this scripture: "And we know that all things work together for good to those who love God, to those who are the called according to His purpose" (Romans 8:28 NKJV). I would soon experience far greater grace from God—grace that would outweigh any challenge I faced in my career because I relied on God for the answers after the sacrifice.

Exactly one year to the date of my miscarriage, God blessed me with two beautiful baby girls. I was promoted to the rank of Captain, the very position that many tried to keep me out of. I now stand confidently in the ranks preparing for my next promotion as well as mentoring and preparing others as they sacrifice.

Once I began to understand that I possessed something that many of those around me lacked, I realized the value of my uniqueness. I began to appreciate my wealth of knowledge as well as the impact that I had on all those around me. The difference in me made a difference and still makes a difference in others. I began to dare myself to be confident in my uniqueness because others did not possess the courage to be different or understand the value of it. So when you begin to feel weighed down, remember that we as women are unique because of our unique sacrifice in the uniform! Embrace your uniqueness, ladies!

"Cast thy burden upon the Lord, and he shall sustain thee: he shall never suffer the righteous to be moved."

—*Psalms 55:22 KJV*

BREAKING THE SPIRIT OF INTIMIDATION

☆ ☆ ☆ ☆ ☆

PATRICIA LAW

Making History

There were times in my military career when I wish I could have gotten out because it was too much for me. But when I began my career, I was young and in a marriage that was falling apart, and we had a baby boy. I had to tough it out. I was a part of history as the last class of the Women's Corp for the Army, better known as the WAC or the Women's Army Corp. What I didn't know was the amount of intimidation I would have to endure as the Army transitioned to an integrated force. I knew through Christ Jesus I would make it, so I trusted God throughout my struggles.

It was a cool day in February 1978 when I began my Army career at Fort McClellan, Alabama. At the age of twenty-six, I was the oldest woman in my class. The other Soldiers ranged from age eighteen to twenty-five. They looked up to me like I was their big sister. I was a natural leader, taking charge when no one else would step up. A little tension arose in our class from another woman who was also twenty-six years old. I believe she was intimidated by me because everyone looked up to me and not her. She always disagreed with whatever I said or tried to do. I would say to myself, *here she comes with that spirit of intimidation; why can't we all work together?*

Once I left Basic Training, I headed to Fort Jackson, South Carolina. I made up my mind that, as Soldiers, we were going to work together. Now, let me remind you that we were the last class of the WAC and we had our dos and don'ts; as women, we couldn't do too much. I was in the food service field, and we had to show our male counterparts that we could do the same job as them and work together. But many of the male Soldiers didn't like that we could do the job better than them, so they were intimidated. They were worried that we would make rank before they would. Our chain of command only saw that the job was done to standard and that they could count on us.

Even though the women proved we could do the job, we were still limited in what we could do. For example, we could not lift over ten pounds, we could not go to the field to help set up the tents, and we could not pick up supplies and equipment. The only thing they wanted me to do was sit behind the typewriter, answer phone calls, do paperwork, order supplies, and turn in finance paperwork to the bank. But when I was recommended for Cook of the Month and Cook of the Quarter, I won. That's when the smart comments started and others' intimidation increased. I heard my male counterparts say things like, "the only thing she does is sit behind the desk" and "we're doing the hard work." The male Soldiers felt intimidated because here I was, some woman in a male-dominated unit, getting special treatment and getting recognized.

During the early part of my career in 1980 to 1982, I made rank pretty quickly and I was put in charge of my male-dominated section at Fort Bliss, Texas. As a clerk, I was working directly with the food service manager, doing worksheets, menus, ordering rations, and going to meetings. I was surprised that I was selected for this position over other Soldiers who had been in the unit longer than me, and I was just a Specialist Four. The leadership saw that women could do the job just as well as men, and that they could depend on us. After I was promoted to Specialist Five and received awards, the male Soldiers were even more intimidated.

Doing My Job

I continued to work hard throughout my military career, not to show my male counterparts up but to show them we could work together to complete the mission. I wanted them to look beyond gender and not be intimidated by us women so we could work together to get the job done. I especially wanted them to see that favor and promotion come from God Almighty. The scripture says in Psalms 75:6 KJV, "For promotion cometh neither from the east, nor from the west, nor from the south."

In 1990 during Desert Storm, intimidation was at a serious high. I was a promotable Staff Sergeant placed in charge of a section of National Guard and Reserve Soldiers. I was placed in this position because I was active duty; it didn't matter that there was a Sergeant First Class or Master Sergeant who outranked me in the section. There was so much tension in the section because of this. They were intimated by me, but I was only focused on doing my job and keeping everybody safe while in combat.

During that deployment, I proved to them that I could get the job done. Our chain of command even took notice. Eventually we all began to work together because they saw that I was there to do a good job, not take anyone's job or position—there was really no reason for them to be intimidated by my being placed in that position. Like them, I was there to do a job and be a part of the team.

As a woman in the US Army, I experienced a great amount of intimidation throughout my career, yet I was still able to rise through the ranks. I sacrificed and overcame a lot for the women who are serving today. When I look back to where I began with the Women Corps in 1978 to today, the Army has come a long way, and it should be proud of the women who serve with distinction and exemplify its highest values. I am excited to see so many opportunities opening up for women, as they continue to play a vital role in the military and serve as assets to the team. Continued integration of women in all career fields will only strengthen the Army's readiness.

TENACIOUS, BLESSED, AND COVERED BY GRACE

☆ ☆ ☆ ☆ ☆

RADIAH MALLARD

Uncertain Beginnings

My beginnings were uncertain. I was unwanted, moved from foster home to foster home where I was abused. I experienced physical, mental, and sexual abuse only to be returned to my abusive mother. My parents were divorced, and I never knew my father. As a by-product of my early life, I became a "people pleaser" because I thought it would buy me the love and affection I so desperately wanted and needed. Over half of my life was spent trying to please others. The other half was spent fighting for my country, my children, and my place in the world.

My first two years of military service were spent as an airman in the Navy. My goal was to complete my two-year enlistment and come home with money for college. As a young Sailor, I was fortunate enough to work with some of the brightest minds in the aircraft mechanic industry. As a three-year student of Mandarin Chinese, I fit in well with these brilliant minds and even considered a career as an interpreter. But with my insecurities and naive view of the world, I instead chose to marry the first person who proposed. He wasn't ready and, years later, I realized I wasn't either.

Within four months of marriage, I was pregnant with my first child. I put my dreams of being an interpreter aside, left the Navy, and went back home. I was accepted into the college I wanted, so I started school and worked two jobs to make ends meet, while my husband was more concerned with video games than fatherhood. I ended up pregnant again with our son. Then at twenty-three, I got the chicken pox. With no health insurance, I was out of work for two weeks. As I nursed myself back to health, I realized that I needed the military in order to provide a better life for my children. I decided that once I was in, I'd make the best of it. And I did just that. Tenacious? Maybe.

In 1997, I joined the Army and was assigned to a Special Operations Support Company. It was there I would spend the next seven years of my life training with men day in and day out. We were family. They were my brothers. During that time, I led company runs, carried men twice my weight up hills and over obstacles, and jumped out of perfectly good aircrafts in high winds. I was blessed with male mentors who respected me, pushed my limits, and challenged me to be greater than I was. I won Department of the Army level awards and received accolades for support, all while having two more children, one of whom was diagnosed with level III autism.

Potential Realized

While I was at work being all that I could be, my husband was getting DUIs, getting arrested, and neglecting marital and financial responsibilities. We lost our home, and on several occasions, I was faced with the possibility of losing my children because of incidents that occurred while I was away at training. By the grace of God, my leadership looked out for me and had my best interests as their priority. I was a good Soldier, and they saw my potential. Eventually, I began to believe that I could do anything I set my mind to. That's when I put in my Warrant Officer packet.

I was the senior ranking Soldier in my field at the time as a young E-5 Sergeant, but I didn't let that stop me. I went to senior Warrant Officers in my field, requested on-the-job training and worked with them three times a week to learn the system I was aspiring to become an expert in. This opened the door for me to receive excellent recommendation letters that got me selected into the Warrant Officer Corps. Tenacious? Possibly.

In 2004, I graduated from Warrant Officer Basic Course (WOBC), moved to a new duty station and was on my way to Iraq with my first platoon of Soldiers. The Army outside of the Special Operations world was new to me; it was a place where funds were low and nothing made sense. There was very little structure and even less teamwork. I felt like a fish out of water at first. Imagine me, a woman, being awkward around other women.

Fortunately, during my first deployment, the majority of my NCOs went about their business, and leadership trusted my expertise—unlike the second tour. During my second deployment, all my fears about working with women were realized. There was gossip, backstabbing, lies, jealousy, and a fierce competitiveness to be noticed. It was so bad that I chose not to socialize, even when I had units to support. This backfired on me, and I was labeled as being difficult. Even though my peers and higher leadership saw outstanding performance in numbers, and units outside of our area of operation would specifically request to be serviced at my warehouse, my Commander viewed me as incompetent. To this day, I still don't know why. When my last deployment was over, I knew two things:

1. I would never let anyone tell me who I was again.

2. Their opinion would never dictate my outcome; I had control of that.

Tenacious? *Absolutely!*

Today, I can look at my past and say that it is a part of me. Between deployments, I got divorced, split my children up between family and friends so they could be safe while I was away, and had a nervous breakdown. In spite of the difficulties I encountered, I still was able to find myself, have a successful career, raise four beautiful children, and marry again after the love of my life found me. We are now the proud owners of a property management franchise and are living out our dreams. I see that God was there all along. It was not easy, but every bit of the struggle made me stronger, more certain, and more *tenacious*.

DUTY TO
SELF

FAITH AND RESILIENCY TO OVERCOME

☆ ☆ ☆ ☆ ☆

ADENA TUFTS

Heart of a Servant

My advice for people in the military is that life will teach you to have faith and resiliency. In my opinion, faith means to trust and know things will work out for your good. Resiliency is the capacity to recover quickly from difficulty. It instills toughness and strength in you. The military taught me that I can endure so many circumstances if I change my perspective and work hard.

I joined the Army in 2007. I always wanted to be in the military, and since I already had a bachelor's degree, my cousin encouraged me to join the Army as an officer. In October of that year, I joined the military as a Nurse Corps Officer. Being a nurse in the military was very difficult as I worked long, tiring hours, but I loved my job, and because I have the heart of a servant, I loved caring for my patients and witnessing their healing. There were many times when I was caring for patients with terminal illnesses that I cried on my way home while praying for their healing.

Throughout my career, I experienced a lot of frustrations within the healthcare system. I used these frustrations to recommend positive changes to the system. I believe it is best to find solutions to the issue instead of just complaining about them, and I learned to develop solutions to issues that occurred. Changing your perspective about situations allows you to come up with different ways to tackle issues. Also, it's important to speak up about certain frustrations. As women, we feel like our voices don't need to be heard. However, if you have an idea about fixing a problem, it's important to bring your perspective to the table. When I started in the military, I did not speak about things that were bothering me. But as I learned the military system and grew comfortable with my peers, I started coming up with solutions to systemic issues that bothered me.

When I joined the military, I did not know what to expect. Throughout my career, I've been around people who have encouraged me and let me know that all things will work out through hard work and doing the right thing. Even as I prepare to transition from active duty to the reserves after being involuntarily separated due to a reduction of force, things are positively working out. If someone told me this a year ago, I would have doubted them, but the military provided me with a lot of tools to move into my next career field. I've obtained skills in leadership, communication, and coaching.

Everything works out for your good. Part of the battle is getting to that point where you know it will work out. So if you are facing an obstacle, know that this obstacle was foreseen and you already have the tools and strength to get through that circumstance. You are equipped to pass every test that's presented to you. You will pass tests and, over time, the right people are placed in your life to equip and empower you to pass tougher tests.

The Army has taught me to become resilient and overcome obstacles. I have not always succeeded at everything I have tried, but being in the military allowed me to see other people's perspectives. I met people from all walks of life, including many strong women. I worked sixty hours a week, completed community service, mentored other Soldiers, and maintained a 4.0 GPA in my master's program—all at the same time. I know that it's all by God's grace. God gives me the strength and resiliency to accomplish these goals.

Praying Nurse

Currently, I am a travel nurse working in a pediatric ICU in Ohio. When I arrived here, although it was my hometown, I did not know what to expect or how nursing in the civilian sector worked. I prayed daily that I would see the presence of God and know that I was walking in His will for my life.

As a traveling nurse, I recently had the pleasure of caring for two families, both of whom were strong in their faith, so we encouraged one another. They were having a difficult time dealing with their child's illnesses, which is understandable. So while caring for these families, I asked if I could pray with them and for them. During my time spent with both families, I felt the presence of God and His love. I felt His heart for them and I continually thanked Him for being there for me, guiding me as I cared for the children, and giving me a heart to love others and have faith that God was with each of us during that time.

Despite my situation of being separated from the military, I had to trust that God was making plans for my life without my knowledge, so I got up every day and went to my job. I could have felt sorry for myself and my situation, but I asked God to change my perspective. That was the best prayer I could have prayed. When God changes your perspective about a situation, you can walk in there and accept and embrace the change.

If things aren't going the way you hoped they would, I pray God changes your perspective. I pray your faith increases and that you understand you are not alone. God has your back and He's covering you every step of the way. I encourage you to embrace your new journey with open arms. I pray that you know that God loves you and He's ordering all your steps, even if they don't make sense to you at the moment. I challenge you to trust Him daily. Write a letter expressing your thoughts and maintain a journal showing how you overcame the obstacle of living life when it didn't go "your way." It's not an accident that you are in the space you are in; learn lessons from it. Embrace life and kick it in the head.

WITH GOD, ALL THINGS ARE POSSIBLE

☆ ☆ ☆ ☆ ☆

CATHY A. GRANT

My Double Life

I can do *all* things with God's help—even survive. I didn't always believe this. I didn't believe because I struggled. I struggled to come to terms with the fact that I was in an abusive marriage. I struggled with my self-esteem and self-worth. I struggled with guilt and shame.

I was about twenty-one years old when I arrived at my first duty station and met *him*. He was older, a little overprotective and controlling, but I concluded this was his way of showing me love. In hindsight, I ignored the warning signs that were present from the beginning.

As our relationship progressed, more signs presented themselves. He isolated me from my friends and even accused me of sleeping with other men. Then, the physical abuse began. He would slap and punch me, and I learned quickly how to camouflage my bruised and swollen body parts. My body, camouflaged to hide his angry blows.

Within a year of marriage, I discovered that I was pregnant. I have always believed that children are a blessing, but I knew I had made a huge mistake by marrying him. I was embarrassed and ashamed. I became depressed and cried a lot, shedding countless tears.

Although I hid this dysfunctional relationship throughout my military career, I made peace with myself. This peace allowed me to escape my situation for a time, if only in my mind. I often wondered, *if the neighbors knew, what would they think?* But I didn't say anything and neither did they. I was too afraid and thought how the situation could take a turn for the worse if outsiders found out or said anything. I wondered if I reported the abuse, would the police believe me? What if they took his side? No, I couldn't chance that, so I chose to protect him instead of reporting his violent behavior. Besides, reporting domestic violence would ruin his career, and I didn't want to do that. It was safer this way—hidden.

My husband was an alcoholic, and I knew that it was only a matter of time before this behavior would catch up with him. While we were stationed in Germany, my husband transitioned and separated from the military. When we returned to the United States, his drinking worsened and so did the fights, attacks, and arguments.

There was no peace in our home. I was an emotional wreck because my mind was flooded with thoughts and questions—*how did I end up here?* My main concern at that point was how I would get my daughter and myself out of that situation.

I worked late nights to stay away from him. I was even happy when it was time for my unit to go to the field for training—crazy, huh? Then I was slammed back into reality when it was time to go home to my horrible life of shame.

The last straw was when he threatened to take half of my military retirement pay if I left him. That was a heavy burden. I couldn't imagine having to give him anything after I had worked so hard in my military career. After the pain and suffering had I endured at his hands—no! He didn't deserve a single penny from me.

Here I was, a Sergeant leading Soldiers in the Army, living this double life. I felt like a complete hypocrite. I was responsible for Soldiers who looked up to me, and here I was allowing my husband to mistreat and disrespect me.

My Moment in the Light

This was a dark time in my life. I didn't have a relationship with God mainly because it was hard for me to trust Him since I couldn't see Him. I grew tired and didn't know what else to do. I didn't care about the money anymore; I just wanted out. I cried out to the Lord with my whole heart and asked Him to help me get out of this marriage. He heard me! The next day, the sheriff knocked on my door and asked for my husband. My husband was being sued for child support by another woman. He claimed he didn't know who this woman was, but I didn't care because I knew that this was my way out. It was over. I had been to hell and back.

Once the divorce was final, I took my life back. I never thought that I would love again, but God sent me an angel who loves me unconditionally, and now I know I am worthy of love because I am more valuable than the finest jewels. I thank God that today I can call myself a survivor of domestic violence because many people don't make it out. I believe God had his angels surrounding me through the whole experience. Now, I am glad to share my story to help others find the courage to leave their abusive situations.

My warning to others is simple: don't ignore the signs. The signs of domestic abuse are often very noticeable. Don't ignore them, make excuses, or take the blame. Often, we choose to protect the abuser for fear of ruining their military career or our own. I would tell anyone facing this difficult decision to get help; your life may very well depend on it. If a man hits you once, most likely, he will do it again.

Lastly, I remind my sisters in arms to look out for each other. We must truly be our sisters' keepers. If you see signs that your battle buddy is being abused, ask questions or report it because it could save their life. I'll be honest—it took me years to admit that I was a victim of domestic violence, but that's not the end of my story. With God's help, I overcame it. I am a survivor and that means you can survive too.

BE WHO YOU ARE

☆ ☆ ☆ ☆ ☆

CSILLA TOTH

Desperate to Fit In

Have you ever felt that you don't belong? That you don't fit in? Have you wondered if you have to change in order to be accepted? I can relate to all of it.

A little red chair.

A dark bedroom's doorway.

The sniffles of young children.

When they fell asleep, their breathing became slower, deeper, and steadier. I sat on that little red chair. We had bought it during one of our first garage sales as we started our journey in the United States. It stayed with us as a reminder of those first days of our new life.

I ended most of my days on that chair, reflecting on the time that unmercifully keeps going. Being a mom, I adored watching my little ones as they slipped into the world of dreams and wonders. They are truly my pride and joy, in the period of their life when I can watch them grow up to become wonderful men and women of God.

When I started my journey in the military, I was excited. I had always wanted to serve since I was a teenager, but I grew up in Hungary, and women were not able to enlist at that time. It was mandatory for all men at the age of eighteen. I told several of my peers I would take their place if I could. I was serious too. I didn't know that years later I would find myself raising my right hand to join the military at the age of thirty-four, just a month before my fifth child turned one year old.

During the next few months of initial training, I realized that I was different in so many ways. I was raised in another country, in a different culture. English was my second language so communication was difficult. I was older than 98 percent of the Soldiers in training with me, just a few years younger than most of their mothers. I was a mother of five children and married for over fifteen years with a bachelor's degree.

When I joined the military, I had hoped to find people like me who were at similar stages in their lives and with similar interests. I wondered if I was ever going to find that group. Would I ever fit in? I believe people bond naturally with others who are at the same phase in life as they are, and I was searching desperately to find that bond.

Unfortunately, I realized there was nothing like that out there for me. I began to wonder if I would have to change radically to be accepted. Being myself caused problems and knocked down my self-esteem over and over again. People misjudged me because of my reserved behavior. They even looked down on me. Over time, I proved them wrong by just being myself and working hard. This was a painful and long process. I just wanted to skip over this rocky road. No one ever wants to feel like nothing. I let other people's opinions of me outweigh my own value of myself.

My Light Bulb Moment

I sat down one day to take an inventory of myself. Who am I? What core values drive my life? I'm Christian, but I'm far from perfect. But biblical principles have been instilled in me since I can remember and I try to do my best every day. I will not change that; I'm certain of it. I'm a wife and a mother, and I will always be because of the love, promises, and blood that hold us together. Family is my motivation. This is imprinted in my life forever.

As I worked to find my identity, I came across a book that encouraged readers to list one hundred positive things about themselves. I made that list and read it out loud. I looked in the mirror and told that person on the other side how wonderful she was. Have you ever been caught talking to yourself in front of a mirror? The person who caught you probably looked at you like you were a little crazy and asked, "Are you talking to yourself?" If you find yourself in this situation, I encourage you to reply like I do: "Yes, I am. I think I'm awesome and easy to talk to." They will either agree or think that you are crazier than they thought. It will at least give you both a good laugh.

I realized that there were things in life that I wanted to do but for some reason I stopped doing them. It was as if I had lost my passion and I wondered if I would ever do them again. I felt lost, like I was in the wilderness walking around without reaching my destination.

One day, as I was driving home from work, I was listening to one of Joyce Meyer's teachings and it spoke to me loud and clear: "You are in the wilderness of your life, working some junk out of you that needs to come out before you will be ready to have what God promised you."

After hearing this message, the light bulb came on. At that moment, I realized I *had* to change. But not the way I thought. I wanted to use my willpower to change in a day or two, but real change comes over time, with hardship and sorrow—the things we want to avoid in life. During life's transformations, we go through a lot of change, but never give up your character or your personality. We all are unique and original. Just be the best version of yourself.

I'm grateful for this season of my life. As a woman in the military, I have to be strong in this male-dominated field, and I am strong-hearted and brave, remaining faithful to my true character while transforming into a better version of myself. And at the end of the day, I find myself guarding the dreams of those precious lives I was created to care for, sitting in the dimly lit bedroom on that little red chair.

THREE TIMES
A CHARM

☆ ☆ ☆ ☆ ☆

DANNIELLE RAMOS RASH

Married to the Military

It was March 1995 in Rhode Island, and I had just turned twenty-one. I had already been serving in the Army National Guard for two and a half years. My experience in the National Guard was so fulfilling to me, I decided to join the ranks and sign up for the active-duty Army. I thought I'd maybe see the world, but not before running to the altar and marrying the "love of my life." Boy, was I wrong! We had only been dating for six months and we were both young and dumb, as the saying goes. After we married, we reported to my first duty station in Fort Lee, Virginia.

Soon after we arrived, my husband began to drink a bit more than usual. One cold and snowy night, my husband

and I went to a dance club with some friends. At the end of the night, we arrived at our house on post, and he began to force himself on me. I told him no and he went into a rage. He threw a shoe at me, and it hit me in the face. I knew I had to get away, so I began packing my bag. He ran toward me and strangled me. I managed to get away from him, and with nothing on but some Army physical fitness shorts and a t-shirt, I ran barefoot out of the house and into the snow. I went to a friend's house nearby and spent the night.

The next morning, I attended formation and my friend and coworker noticed the mark on my face and neck. She knew instantaneously what had happened, and she reported it to the First Sergeant. And so began the family advocacy appointments. Those appointments only lasted a few months before I came down on a hardship tour to Korea. After a few months on my own in Korea, I made up my mind to get a divorce. I realized my husband was weighing me down and I had no future with him. It wasn't until I landed at my next duty station that it was finalized.

Twice Is Nice...Not

After Korea, I reenlisted for a three-year tour to Hawaii. I was ecstatic because Hawaii had been my first choice for a duty station! In January 1997, I landed on the lovely island of Oahu. I would spend two tours in paradise. About a year after being stationed in Hawaii, I met husband number two.

My second husband was in the Army as well, and again, we married very quickly. This marriage lasted from 1998 to 2002.

Once again, the Army had other plans for me and I came down on orders to Louisville, Kentucky. My husband was pending a medical board and stayed in Hawaii. However, by this time, I had my son, my little "pineapple," to think of. I relocated to Kentucky and stayed in the Army another eight months before I transitioned out. My husband had basically dropped all communication with my son and me since we had left Hawaii.

I continued to work full-time and attend school full-time. I was determined to obtain a college education. The university looked at my husband's finances, and my financial aid advisor stated that if I wasn't married, I could get the full grant for school. Despite him not sending any money to assist his child or myself, I still couldn't receive the full grant unless I was divorced. After about a year and a half in Kentucky, while attending the University of Louisville, I sought out an attorney and filed for a divorce. At that point, I felt like a huge failure.

This One Is a Keeper

It was 2003, and I had no desire to have a boyfriend or get involved with any man. My sole focus was on my son and my education. I spent most days and nights at home and on the computer doing homework. This was the year chat rooms were popular. I met a man online and he lived in Washington, D.C. We emailed and instant messaged each other every day and occasionally visited one another. He was eleven years my senior. We fell into a long-distance relationship. I kept telling myself I would never move for a man, however, at the time, my boyfriend had a job in D.C. and the jobs in Kentucky were not really what I wanted.

Fast forward to 2006, I graduated college and relocated to the D.C. area a week after. I figured with my military background, Washington, D.C., would be the perfect place for me. I'm so happy I made that decision! I learned from my prior mistakes. We dated for a year and a half and lived together for a year and a half prior to tying the knot. He treats my son as if he was his own, and I am happy to report that we have been through ten years of wedded bliss. After over thirteen years of being together, we are both still in love as if it were the first day we met.

In the end, I'm glad I went with my gut and relocated to the D.C. area. Despite the turmoil in my failed marriages, I am glad I went through it and have learned from my past failed marriages. My advice to others is to take the time to get to know the person who you will spend the rest of your life with, and be more selective in your life partners. Do not settle! Occasionally, when I'm with family and friends, they joke and call me Elizabeth Taylor or Zsa Zsa Gabor. I laugh at it and say, "I would rather get out of a bad marriage than stay and be miserable for the rest of my life." Life is truly about love—loving yourself and loving each other.

My mother always told me, "Sometimes you have to kiss a few frogs to find your prince." Boy, was she right.

A CHANGE OF PLANS

☆ ☆ ☆ ☆ ☆

DIANE MOSLEY

Life's Direction

Call it a dream or call it reality, but my plan for my life changed without my consent. My life's plan did not account for others being in disagreement. But through it all, I have a better understanding of Romans 8:28 KJV: "And we know that all things work together for good to them that love God, to them who are the called according to his purpose."

It was my plan and dream to marry and have four boys. I was married fresh out of high school, living independently with my husband, the military Soldier. I dreamed I would go to college, and my husband and I would live the life. Love was supposed to be the recipe for life. Call it being naive or innocent, but neither life nor marriage went as I expected.

There were a lot of new adventures and avenues that were unfamiliar to and unexplored by my husband and me. We moved to Honolulu, Hawaii, and I wanted to see everything the island had to offer. We had the financial resources, and I was using them, visiting every beach and store. My husband was advancing in his military career. We were enjoying life. As we explored new things, our focus on marriage slowly faded. There were places to go and things to see. Things I no longer needed permission from my mom to do. I started working and I liked the financial independence. We had even more financial resources to live our lives. My husband did not mind; he was busy enjoying life just the same. But our interests were not the same, and even though we lived in the same house, our activities rarely included each other. We focused more on our individual desires or our friends' desires. We were unaware and lacked the know-how to notice that our marriage was fading.

About two years after high school, my interest in attending college resurfaced. Unlike the first time we discussed my going to college, my husband was not supportive about paying for college. No big deal, I thought. I had a job. But I was clueless about the college experience and unfamiliar with loans, Pell grants, and financial aid. However, I knew several military Soldiers and family members who were attending or had graduated from college, and they gave me guidance and direction with the process. Most of my maternal family members had not finished high school, but I was motivated because on a regular basis I saw young military men and women living independently, and some were even in leadership roles. I aspired to do the same.

During college, the support from my husband was lacking at times, but my military friends pitched in and provided support, which was priceless. We had become family. These were not friends whom I had known all my life; they were friends connected through the bond of the military, and their support assisted me in maneuvering through many difficulties.

A New Plan

During my sophomore year, my husband decided he was going to transition out of the military. We were excited about starting fresh. I was working as a secretary on the military base, so I applied to transfer my job to another military base closer to our hometown. I accepted a job offer, and off I went. My husband stayed behind to complete his enlistment. My move went smoothly, but at the end of my husband's enlistment, he changed his mind and reenlisted in the military. At that point, we were living apart in two different states. Since I had already accepted the position, moved to the new military base, and enrolled in college, we decided I should stay and finish my degree. Even though our marriage had hit some challenges, we thought we would be fine living apart until I finished college. But while pursuing my college degree, our marriage unraveled, and by the time I graduated, we were no longer married.

A few months after graduation, I was offered a new career opportunity. I accepted the position and, without trepidation, moved to a major city. I was better prepared for life because of the things I had learned during my time affiliated with the military. All credit goes to God. He used the military to change my outlook on life.

This new position created my own identity. I was no longer identified by my military ID card but by my profession. For me, the military exposed me to so many windows of opportunity and multiple individuals to show me the way along my journey. Challenges came and went, but my military support never wavered. Today, I still work for the government, but I am no longer a secretary. Today, I am one of those professionals I aspired to be, just without the husband and the four sons. Even though my life plan changed, my military experience has proven to be invaluable. I truly believe every situation worked together for my good.

GOD'S SAVING GRACE

☆ ☆ ☆ ☆ ☆

DONNA RAMIREZ

My Journey

My story begins when I was born in 1960 to a single teenage mother. Between my mother being a workaholic and choosing to always work or party, I felt like a motherless child much of my childhood. Since my mother was not around much, my brother, sister, and I lived with our grandmother in her two-story log cabin home. Despite this, we loved our mother and mourned her passing from stage four breast cancer—just eight days shy of her seventy-first birthday. I mark her death as another significant turning point in my story.

When I was a small child, I loved to play outside. One day, my brother, sister, a few cousins, and I decided to rake the leaves into a pile and set them on fire. The fire grew fast, grew too big, and got too close to the house, setting the house on fire. Unfortunately, my baby cousin was sleeping inside the house. Our mother was driving up to the house after returning from work and saw the fire. She ran into the house and rescued our great-grandmother, but she was unable to save my baby cousin. My mother suffered third-degree burns on her stomach and chest.

As a result of the fire, my siblings and I were shuffled around once again and ended up moving into our grandfather's home; he was a mean old man who did not want us there. We had to stay outside all day until it was time to go to bed and we were served meals through a window. People started talking about our situation, saying that we were being neglected, which resulted in a report being made to social services. Soon after, a caseworker showed up and placed us in a Volkswagen Beetle and took us away. More shuffling around for my siblings and I, this time in the foster system. My sister and I were placed together in a foster home, and my brother was placed in a home with our cousins.

The first foster home I was placed in, I was sexually and mentally abused for three months. It was terrible—something a child should never have to experience. We then moved out of that home and into another foster home with an older couple who we called Granny and Pappy. Granny taught us to read and write, and we memorized the Bible. She was a very strict parent, and we spent most of our extra time cleaning and cooking. I knew she cared about us, but she never told us she loved us. Pappy was an alcoholic; he came home drunk every weekend. He was very fresh—I guess some would call him a "dirty old man"—but he never touched us in an inappropriate manner.

Looking for Love

As we grew older, on several occasions, my sister and I would sneak out of Granny and Pappy's house to try to find love in all the wrong places. My sister ended up pregnant and moved out. At that point, I decided I needed a change in my life. I had two choices: go to Bible college or join the US Army. I made the choice to serve my country.

I attended Basic Training at Fort Jackson, South Carolina, and was then stationed at Fort Stewart, Georgia. My job in the Army was 94B, which is a cook. I felt I was the best cook, especially at stewing. I made the best of my new life in the Army. While working on the food serving line, there was this one particular Soldier who would always tease me and make me laugh. He was tall, dark, and handsome and spoke broken English. From our first encounter, he would always tell me that I was going to become his wife. I would ignore him, but he was very persistent. Eventually, he won me over. He treated me like a lady and had such great manners. I fell in love with him, and he became my king. We married in 1980 before being stationed in Germany.

After having three children, I decided to transition out of the military, retiring with an honorable discharge. I am grateful for my time in the military because it was my escape from my past and it is where I met my wonderful husband. My husband and I have been married for thirty-six years now. I feel like I have come a long way from the challenges I faced in my childhood. What has kept me focused over the years has been my church family. I am involved in different programs at my church, which has truly been my saving grace, and I volunteer with the mission soup kitchen and the nursing home ministry.

When I look back over my life, I can say that I have overcome many stumbling blocks and made it through several setbacks. I survived! I look at the challenges I went through in my lifetime, things that could have easily broken my spirit—loss of my mother, sexual abuse, physical abuse, mental abuse, neglect, and separation from my siblings—and I know that I made it through for a reason. It is by God's grace that I survived. I give all praise and glory to God because without Him, I would have never made it. I know it is because of Him that I have lived to tell about it. I am a survivor.

MY LIFE BEHIND THE COVER

☆ ☆ ☆ ☆ ☆

EBONY JOHNSON

Bound by the Curse

My life has been full of twists and turns. I've always been resilient. I became a master cover girl, able to hide the pain and quietly pick up the pieces to rebuild. At the tender age of fifteen, I survived a brutal rape by a serial rapist. I screamed for help as bystanders stood by and refused to step in to stop the rape. My rapist, who was in his mid-thirties and a stranger to me, told the bystanders that it was a "domestic issue." I pleaded with them to help me, yet they all watched me get raped and did nothing.

The rape was a defining moment in my life. For years, I internalized my pain and suffered from low self-esteem and depression. I felt that I didn't deserve to be loved and that I didn't have a voice. I entered one bad relationship after another. I signed up for the US Air Force Delayed Enlistment Program at the age of seventeen and enlisted in January 1998. I needed to escape my hometown of Philadelphia to find my pathway to healing. I served honorably for fourteen years and met people who I now consider my brothers and sisters in arms. Over the years, I was able to travel the world. I've been stationed in Hawaii and overseas in Korea and Germany, and I was deployed to Afghanistan.

The worst memory of my deployment to Afghanistan was the day we experienced a fire in our housing unit and a bomb attack during a VIP visit. We lost twenty-three of our comrades that day. It was devastating, but we all stood tall during the silent drill ceremony to pay tribute to our fallen friends.

When I returned home from deployment, I had difficulties adjusting back to normal life. It was hard connecting to people and being emotionally present in relationships. I had difficulties dealing with supervisors and leadership. I often shut down and desired to be left alone. My family and friends said that I had changed. I suffered from post-traumatic stress disorder (PTSD) and major depression. My life as I once knew it would never be the same. I had to seek help to readjust and move forward. I still struggle to feel normal and free, but I consistently do the work and seek treatment.

Early in my Air Force career, I received a phone call and was informed that my aunt was murdered at the hands of her ex-boyfriend, whom she had a protective order against. He violated the protective order, went to her apartment, and with my cousins present, shot her through the door. I flew back home to be with my family and mourn the loss of my aunt due to domestic violence. A few years earlier, another aunt was killed in a murder-suicide at the hands of her boyfriend. I desired to break the cycle of domestic violence on my family and made a promise to myself that I would never put my hands on my partner or stay in an abusive relationship.

Even though I made this promise to myself, I still made poor choices in my relationships for years to follow. While overseas in the Air Force, when I was twenty-one, I eloped and married a man thirteen years my senior. After one year of marriage, I learned that my husband had two children who he had failed to claim, and he owed substantial money in back taxes and unpaid child support. My husband eventually became abusive, and I had to flee my home in the middle of the night.

Because my husband was a civilian and considered my military dependent, it was difficult to get any help. I told the police I was afraid for my life. The military police told me he was my problem, and the civilian police refused to get involved. Eventually, my leadership stepped in, and my husband was charged and found guilty of assault, sentenced to six months of probation, and barred from the military installation. I ultimately filed for divorce from him after a year of separation.

Breaking Free from the Curse

Later in life, I found myself in an abusive relationship once again. This was right at a pivotal point in my life when I was facing major health concerns and had recently separated from the Air Force. I fought through the disappointment and hurt when the courts failed to hold my abusive boyfriend accountable. Not only did he physically assault me by choking and hitting me, but he also continuously violated the protective order and stalked me at my place of employment and my home. I was forced to resign my position and relocate to a safe place. He was law enforcement, and I was asked by his defense attorney, "Why do you want to send him to jail?"

I was the victim but was made to feel guilty for holding my abuser accountable for his actions. They sought to protect him because he worked in law enforcement, and they failed to protect me, the victim.

Healing from the abuse, transitioning jobs, and fighting the court systems was a difficult period in my life. During this transition, I completed eighteen months of faith-based discipleship class; Bossed Up Bootcamp, where I learned to navigate a career transition like a boss; and the Boulder Crest Retreat Warrior PATHH (Progressive and Alternative Training for Healing Heroes) program.

Through all of the trials that I faced, my faith never wavered. I picked up the pieces and rebuilt my life. I separated from the US Air Force with an honorable discharge in 2012. I founded The Next Chapter Corporation in 2014, a 501c3 nonprofit dedicated to empowering victims of domestic violence and sexual assault. In 2016, I launched my second business, Success Creators, where we provide career coaching and business development coaching to those in need. Once I opened that door to healing and wellness, the doors opened for me to follow my passion in helping others.

I have lived my life behind the cover for so long, but sharing my story has allowed me to move from behind the cover and use my voice to help others heal. I hope that my story can give strength to other survivors. I want those who are suffering in silence to know that it is possible to pick up the pieces.

WHERE THE PAIN BEGAN

☆ ☆ ☆ ☆ ☆

KALEN ARREOLA

Floating

I was thinking about how beautiful the water looked as I let myself sink down to the bottom of the pool. The summer light was shining through the water as I swam around enjoying the feeling of weightlessness—something I hadn't felt for quite some time.

Things in my life had been tough for a girl of fourteen. My mother went to the hospital, and a week later she was dead. I still had so many things to learn about life, being a woman, love—all the things that happen during the dash. The dash of your life that sits on your tombstone saying you lived 19XX–19XX. My mother's dash was between 1961 and 1995, and I will be forever changed because of it. If only I could have predicted all of the walls I would build around my heart to hide the pain of losing her, and the secrets I would keep to stay sane.

She became my mother at nineteen years old, unwed and blissfully unaware of what was to come. Her story was one of hardship from birth, but her dash was cut short, and the only comforting thought for me was that she was no longer in pain.

I knew she was sick when I was eight, but I had no idea that she would die, or how it would fracture my insides and change the course of my life. Age thirty-three is so young, and we had made plans. We had planned to build out that master bedroom upstairs when she came home; the gladiolas were next. We had to take them out of the garden before it got too cold. But then all I could see was her lifeless body in a hospital bed with tubes coming out from every place, bandages on her head to fix the stroke, and us trying to wake her up with poking and talking and tears coming down so hard that I ran out of them.

And then it hit me.

I had been under the warm, blue water for a very, very long time. The warmth of the water turned dark and cold. I started to feel as though I could not breathe and the weight of the world and the water was closing in. My chest tightened up, and I panicked, looking around for the edge of the pool, but every turn I made, there was nothing but endless water that kept going into the darkness.

Minutes felt like hours as I struggled to swim to the top of the water, but it was too far away. I started to fade, and I knew it was all going to be too late. I was definitely going to die. I took a deep breath in and surrendered to the darkness of the water.

Everything went black.

I gasped as I sucked in a huge breath of air and sat up in my bed. I was dripping with sweat and shaking with fear. Another night of sleeplessness was in full swing, and another night of that nightmare playing on repeat.

Diagnosed with PTSD before it was common to say so, I shoved all the tears down deep and moved on with my life. Worked all day, started drinking, partied whenever possible. But I was fourteen and I was drowning.

The Tide Turns

Fast forward to 2001 when I married my best friend. I have no idea which one of us thought it was a good idea to get married. I knew I could not imagine my life without him. I'll admit, I was codependent in an unhealthy way and I wanted to go wherever he went. He and I discussed getting married and it was done. He gave me a ring when he got home from

Basic Training; it was just like my mother's ring, a marquise cut diamond that I loved.

Two hundred and fifty people came to the ceremony. They sent us off on a journey that I would never really return from. It was an exciting adventure, an escape from the sadness. My young husband didn't have a clue how dead I was inside, but I convinced myself this would make me happy.

He joined the Army and that meant we were leaving the small town we lived in. I told myself all of it was going to be fine. It was peacetime, and if he stayed in until retirement, we would be okay. He always knew he wanted to join the Army and nothing was going to stop him. My painful memories could stay behind as I started a new life with him in a new place, Clarksville, Tennessee, home of the 101st Airborne Division at Fort Campbell.

We married. We moved. We worked. We partied. We were the typical young military couple with no clue about marriage. And then 9/11 happened.

It was time to ship out because the invasion of Iraq was underway. I was 100 percent confident that my husband would die, just like my mother. Rational thought? No. But it was absolutely my truth at that moment.

So I worked. I drank a lot. I was alone. I was "fine." The truth is that I didn't care about my life, so I drank to escape. I betrayed many of my friends, and some of them returned the favor. I just kept on going, continuing to tell myself that I was fine, until it was obvious to everyone else that I wasn't. Thankfully, someone in the heavens was looking out for me, and I made it out of the dark. Looking back, it actually feels like it was another life lived in another world.

I joined the Army Reserves in 2003 and experienced my own deployment and personal healing journey. Things began to make sense. The military gave me confidence, a purpose, and a career path, and things I'd gone through in my early years gave me the ability to help military friends with their PTSD. Although mistakes were made, and things happened that I can never take back, I came out stronger. I value my life, I value my relationships, and I have amazing people around me who love and value me too.

BEAUTY AND THE BEAST

☆ ☆ ☆ ☆ ☆

SOPHIA L. ELLIS

The Beast—Depression and Anxiety

When I was younger, I never felt beautiful. Or important. Or even appreciated. I just knew I existed. However, this never stopped me from living life, being in relationships, or having friends. I knew I was smart. Book smart. Or so I thought. I skipped school to avoid being bullied for being gay. The school board kicked me out of school due to attendance even though I was turning in all my assignments and maintaining a 3.8 GPA.

Luckily, I was able to join the Army Reserves in 2002 at the age of seventeen, with the promise that I would complete my general educational development (GED) before graduating Advanced Individual Training (AIT). So before I was an adult, I learned how to fight for a country. Before I could vote, I fought for those who could vote. Before I was a woman, I was a warrior. Because I was young, naive, and sheltered, my path was hard, bumpy, and misguided.

I never knew that there was even a term for how I have always felt. I just knew that people would look at my accomplishments and tell me how blessed I was—but I didn't feel that way. I felt like it was World War III inside my head, twenty-four hours a day, seven days a week. Bad thoughts of separation and repressed childhood memories constantly ran through my mind. Most days, I didn't feel like myself.

I felt like everyone knew me, but no one saw me.

According to ADAA.org, *depression* is a condition in which a person feels discouraged, hopeless, unmotivated, or disinterested in life in general. *Anxiety disorder* is characterized by persistent, excessive, and unrealistic worry about everyday life.

My anxiety originally surfaced during my first deployment. It was my first time away from home and even though I was not in a "danger" zone (I was in Kuwait), I was frequently troubled with "what ifs." The things I learned in Basic Training and Advanced Individual Training kept me on edge. *Never miss movement. Stay alert, stay alive. Keep your head low. Move, move, move.*

The haunting words from training continued to follow me into my civilian life after deployments and training. While most were able to adapt, this system of training played tricks on my psychological state. The materialistic things became a mask used to hide the emptiness inside; however, there was not enough shopping, makeup, or monthly vacations that could fill the void I was feeling.

Alcohol became my best friend. It took me away from my thoughts and helped me to escape from myself. Most service members suffer from the same thing. I felt like they understood and helped me cope with the beast that resided within. It got so bad that I would look forward to my pre-planned drunken nights. The only thought in my mind was, I would not be myself for at least one weekend. I just wanted a weekend off from myself. From the depression. From life. My drunken nights became so normal that I labeled myself an "alcoholic."

Despite these feelings and my unhealthy manner of coping with them, I was still able to accomplish a lot in my life over the years. I completed my bachelor's and master's degrees in business and established my business brands. Even with all these achievements, I felt nothing. The Army didn't help, either. Prolonged promotions, no acknowledgment for my efforts, and no awards. I was just a body in a formation. I was never suicidal, but I think feeling worthless and helpless is even worse.

My behavior turned more reckless as I found other coping methods to handle my depression: sex. I knew this was the one thing that would get me some attention, and I was good at it. I felt like I had found the cure to my loneliness. Until it began to have a negative impact on my career: late nights and missed days of work.

I couldn't let depression or my recklessness ruin my career. I was still trying to fill the emptiness in my soul, but nothing was working. Worst of all, my cries for help fell on deaf ears and blind eyes. No one stepped in to see what was going on with me.

The Beauty—Perfectly Flawed

Then *it* happened. I found out I was pregnant. God had blessed me with a seed of life. I had always wanted a child. Several doctors told me that I would never get pregnant because I was diagnosed with polycystic ovarian syndrome (PCOS), but here I was, pregnant and excited. My anxiety disorder kicked in and I ended up visiting the OB/GYN five times in two months before my unit's annual training at Fort Devens, Massachusetts.

Who would have known that only one of us would make it back to home station?

At nineteen weeks pregnant, I miscarried my baby boy on November 12 in the hotel bathroom. This hurt me to my soul. My only comfort was knowing that everything happens according to God's timing. That event in my life was a turning point for me. I learned that life is important and I must value it just as God valued me; just as He values us.

The beauty of a woman is the ability to bounce back in the face of adversity. This is my strength as well as yours. I want to encourage you to walk in your strength. Face each day knowing that nothing formed against you will prosper, and we are more than conquerors. You were built for greater, and you are powerful beyond measure. Know that you can do anything you want to accomplish. Don't allow your temporary status to tamper with your permanent peaceful purpose.

I now recognize what I have and am no longer afraid to hide it. The military has a tendency to label anxiety disorder as a common diagnosis and prescribe drugs to disguise the problem. But I made a choice not to sweep it under the rug but embrace my flaw. I appreciate the process of learning about my flaws because it has taught me that I am still God's creation, and He makes no mistakes. In His eyes, I am flawless.

I leave you with one of my daily affirmations: "Queen, you are beautiful and a masterpiece because I am a piece of the Master, our God. You came from royalty and nothing can stop you."

"I praise you because I am fearfully and wonderfully made; yours works are wonderful, I know that full well."

—Psalms 139:14 NIV

Stay beautifully blessed, my queens.

THE DEAFENING SOUND OF SILENCE

☆ ☆ ☆ ☆ ☆

DR. TAMARA P. WILLIAMS

Headed for Self-Destruction

I served in the US Air Force from 2002 to 2006. I enlisted in the military after graduating from Central Michigan University, one month after the attack of September 11, 2001. I entered the military a college graduate with a goal in mind: to continue my education. I was at a point where I knew I had to do something, but I didn't know what. I wasn't ready for the workforce. In retrospect, entering the military was one of the greatest opportunities presented to me at the time. The experience did not start that way; but what came out of the turmoil was a great gift.

Coming from a big city, Washington, D.C., I was out of my element when I entered the military. It was lonely at first, but then I began to meet people. I spent most of my enlistment in Tucson, Arizona, which was very different from the city life I was used to. As an introvert who had already been away from my family for four years, the distance under the new structure began to weigh on me. Although I came from a close family, I was always quiet and reserved. I often felt alone even when people were around.

I carried this behavior with me and quickly learned that the military was about comradery. Being an introvert made it difficult for me to make close friends, but knowing that I had to keep quiet about a significant part of my identity made me feel alone, like I did not fit in and like I had no one to talk to. I was in a long-distance relationship with my girlfriend from college. Military life and the distance became too much, and a year and a half into my enlistment, our relationship ended. This breakup really took a toll on me. I had to go through it alone since I could not share that part of my life with anyone around me. I had to internalize how I was feeling and move on the best way I could while going to work every day.

While I was recovering from the breakup, my grandfather passed away. I flew home for the funeral and was able to spend a few days with my family. It was comforting to see my family even though I was home for a funeral. While home, I found out that my eight-year-old nephew was dying from a rare autoimmune disease. This was difficult to deal with, but I had to return to work. The following month, exactly one month to the day, I received notification that my oldest brother died. And just like that, I was on my way back home for another funeral. This time, I was crushed. My grandfather was old and had been sick for a while, but my brother's death was sudden, and losing him devastated me. I boarded the plane in uniform and the pilot greeted me. He asked how I was doing and I said, "I'm headed to my second funeral in one month."

He put his hand on my shoulder and said, "I'm sorry for your loss."

That moment is forever imprinted in my brain. I felt like I never had time to recover because it was one loss after another. I just remember thinking life wasn't fair.

I stopped caring about everything. I had a difficult time adjusting. I hated going to work every day and didn't want to be around people. I became argumentative. I had trouble sleeping because I worked a twelve-hour night shift. This was when I turned to drinking regularly. My unit became concerned when I showed up for work late one evening. That was the first time my First Sergeant became concerned and recommended that I get help.

That was the turning point. And not only was that the lowest point in my military career, but it was also one of the lowest moments in my life. I was miserable and I knew something had to change. I had one of two choices: continue living in solitude, depressed and mourning, or accept the help that was being offered to me. I accepted the help.

Coming Out of the Dark

I received counseling with a therapist and connected with a power greater than myself. I eventually opened up to someone about how I was feeling. I relied heavily on God and strengthened my faith. For the first time in a long time, I felt like I could share what was going on inside. Although I began to share my struggles with others, I was careful not to mention anything about my sexuality. "Don't ask, don't tell" was the official policy on homosexuality so I could not take any chances. I had to remain silent so I would not risk losing my career.

I eventually enrolled in a graduate program at Troy University, and I came out of my shell even more. Finding the time to do what I wanted while on active duty made all the difference. I began to feel as if I was accomplishing something. Through school, I met more people and even started having fun with my coworkers. I built friendships that I have to this day. I graduated with a master's degree before leaving the military and am proud to say that I have completed a doctorate degree using the GI Bill.

While in school, because I focused on myself and my needs, I began to come out of the darkness of depression. Not only did I have what I believe now to be an awakening, but I learned valuable lessons from that experience that I carry with me today. The awakening came when I realized the importance of connecting with people and how powerful connections can be. I learned that when I get to the point where I am isolating myself and wallowing in self-pity, I need to talk to someone. I also realized that I must do things that feed my spirit; this is necessary for progress. I cannot be afraid to admit something is wrong. I must seek help. Low moments in life create instances for opportunities and it is my duty to identify them in my life.

TRANSITION TO BETTER DAYS

☆ ☆ ☆ ☆ ☆

TAWANDA HARRIS

"And after you have suffered a little while, the God of all grace, who has called you to his eternal glory in Christ, will himself restore, confirm, strengthen, and establish you."

—*1 Peter 5:10 ESV*

Transitions Are a Part of Life

Whether you become a victim of sexual assault, lose a loved one, or experience divorce, financial devastation, problems with your health, catastrophic injury, abuse, or other life-altering events, transitions are a part of life. They are unavoidable. Some transitions are easy and predictable, while other times, we are faced with life-altering changes we'd never envision for our lives.

As harsh and candid as this might sound, it's not helpful to feel sorry for yourself or harbor resentment. Truthfully, it doesn't help us grow past the pain; instead it keeps us there. The most important thing to take away from your transition is spiritual growth. Maybe you've prayed about something and in order for you to receive your answer, you had to go through your ordeal. Some things we will never know the answer to, but we do know that God allowed it to happen, and His purpose is beyond our control. I personally believe transitions occur mainly to help and encourage others. But if you haven't reached spiritual growth or maturity in an area, how can you adequately help someone else who's going through the same ordeal?

I have gone through a major transition myself. From the outside, all seemed bleak and too hard to bear. And to be honest, it was just as bleak and unbearable on the inside. If I were asked to write about this a year ago, it would have been impossible. I was still in a state of distress. However, now that I've suffered a while, I can offer nuggets concerning how my disbelief turned to joy.

My Unexpected Transition

God truly blessed me abundantly. I had a successful military career and was ranked at the top of my field. I was extremely healthy and athletic, running and hiking several miles during the week. I was blessed with wonderful friends and, to top things off, I had recently married the love of my life. Things were really looking up for me, and I was extremely grateful.

Then my life abruptly changed. I suffered a devastating surgical injury, and I was medically discharged from the military. My career was over! I had debilitating nerve injuries, so-called friends waned, and my marriage was badly strained. Many thoughts gripped my mind. I was more confused than anything. My transition was totally unexpected. I never saw it coming. *What was I going to do?*

At the time, I certainly was not thinking about who I could help as I myself was struggling to make it through my ordeal. I began to pray as usual. For days, I could not hear a single word from God. Days turned into months and still nothing. One day, out of the blue, I recalled a quote a friend shared with me over dinner months prior to my injury.

"The teacher never talks during the test," she had said.

I thought, okay, God, *what must I learn during this period of transition*? What would You like me to do? Who would You like me to help? How do I receive Your favor? Where do I go from here?

If you have undergone a major life change like me, you probably also suffered with emotions such as self-doubt, fear, confusion, and anxiety. Maybe you asked God some of the same questions I did. I share my story in hopes of encouraging you during your period of transition. I pray that each of you will be strengthened by the power of the Lord's might and will press through your difficult time.

My Transition to Joy

This experience taught me that it's okay to mourn what I lost for a while, but after some time, I had to get up, set some new goals for myself, and get moving. I realized that as a child of God, I would go through challenges. God allowed those challenges for a specific purpose and, ultimately, it was for my good (Romans 8:28). Remember, despite what you might feel at the time of your transition, God does love you. I had to remind myself of this. He sent His son to overcome every attack we will ever experience during our lifetime. "I have told you all this so that you may have peace in me. Here on earth you will have many trials and sorrows. But take heart, because I have overcome the world" (John 16:33 NLT). I know that no matter what I've lost, when I place my faith in God, He will restore back to me more than I could ever imagine (Ephesians 3:20; 1 Peter 5:10 NIV).

If you feel like hope is lost or if you are struggling with guilt from something that you believe you caused for yourself, this promise is for you too! Isn't that good news? We can believe everything God says about us, His children. You have more to lose if you don't try Him than you would ever lose if you do.

Ponder this question: *After you've suffered a bit, why would God promise to restore you if He did not have a purpose and a plan for you?*

During tough times, I asked myself that question, and it always led me to a place where I took my eyes off my circumstance and placed them on God's promise to restore me. When I think of the word "restore," I think to reestablish, repair, rebuild, and renew. My transition is not over. The injuries I sustained are still very real in my life. If you are also in the midst of a devastating transition that you have yet to overcome, don't lose hope. I learned that it's vital that we make a choice to rejoice because of God's promises to us instead of wallowing in our circumstance. Plus, it's quite draining, don't you think? Instead, I consider that there is a purpose for all I have gone through. To strengthen, restore, and mature me for something greater; perhaps to encourage and uplift someone else. He has a plan for each one of us and it will come to pass (Philippians 1:6).

FIGHTING THE GOOD FIGHT

☆ ☆ ☆ ☆ ☆

TC JORDAN

Fighting to Survive

As I'm writing this, it is a cool breezy afternoon and the sun is beating down on me on this beautiful island of Guam. This Jersey girl raised by a beautiful Southern woman was taught to fight and persevere. I never knew what that truly meant until I joined the military. The joining was easy, signing the contract was easy, but the fighting was hard.

The "Let me tell you that's not right and not because I am black, but because it's wrong" fight was hard. The "I can't keep quiet because you are dealing with people's lives" fight was hard. The "I am a black woman who is not afraid to speak up when everyone else is silent, but you see me as too aggressive when I say it" fight was hard. The "How dare I not be afraid to stand up against the lack of integrity" fight was hard. But I won them all.

The sun shining on my face on this beautiful island lets me know that the fight was not in vain. While fighting for the right to be who I am without apologizing, without compromising, without breaking my integrity, without breaking down and showing weakness, I began to change the focus of the outcomes from my fight. My fight became one of positive change, where I could see a smile appear from feeling like I'd been heard, believed, and headed on the road in the right direction. I was fighting for those who couldn't speak because of fear. I was fighting for those victims of sexual assault when they couldn't stand against the accused, the ranks, and the system. I was their voice, I was their strength, I was their shield. I believed in them, and I was their beacon to assist them in finding the way to their inner voice. Then I built them up, which allowed them to fly free to begin their own fight on fairer grounds.

I always wondered why I had to fight, to endure the pains, to endure the lies, and why I should allow people to make me feel out of touch with my sanity or be accused of being too passionate. These battles, as I like to call them, were rooted in many origins that branched out. However, the battles never failed to hit the paths of my being a woman, being black, not knowing my place others had set for me, and most of all being confused as to why all the previous paths mattered anyway.

Did the fight leave me bitter, broken, and out of sorts? Did it cause me to be regretful or even wish that people saw me differently? Sadly, for a short time, it did. I wondered why the ones who didn't know their job were always winning awards or pressing forward when their work was often split or handled by those of us who did. I wondered why the white females and males who were wrong felt so offended and disrespected, and claimed to be in fear when they were told the truth about themselves. I wondered why, when I was asked a question regarding their expertise on a subject, if they were correct in a statement they made, or if I agreed with a statement they made. I was often met with anger and disappointment when I told the truth.

Fighting for My Future

So how did I move forward? First, I decided right then and there who I was. I was determined to never let that go again and to be ready to defend and stand up for myself when it was required, even if I had to do it in silence by pressing forward and allowing them to watch who I was. Second, I turned down the noise. The noise of those who didn't appreciate who I was and what I stood for. The noise of the money—the thought that I had to make a choice to follow what the money would do for me instead of what I needed to do for myself—often led me to make poor choices. The noise of those who wanted to convince me that their way was better and I would be left in ruins if I left the military because that is what always happened. Third, I focused. I focused on what was important to me and what I wanted. I focused on who I wanted to see when I looked in the mirror and how much it would affect me to not see her on a daily basis. Lastly, I researched. I researched and discovered what it would take for me to be who I drove to be! I researched what I needed to be the best me in the area that I chose.

All of that fighting and winning after I thought I had lost showed me exactly who I was. A leader. A strong leader, set up all nicely packaged in the visionary presence of a black woman. I had it—the compassion, the understanding, the patience, the reasoning, and the empathy to lead—so I did. I opened up my own path to present my talents.

I created Xokiahi Cares, Inc., an unconventional non-profit setup to assist people in their time of need, for all of their needs. We seek out those issues for which we can create a solution for people. No questions asked, no obligation, and no judgment. I run it, and the battles I endured help me to understand what those who are working for me may feel and how they need to be understood, encouraged, and told the truth, no matter how it may hurt either party. I focus on the reason why I do it and that is to help others. By keeping my focus on my purpose, I can say that I did not stand in my own way and I did not allow those around me to change my spirit or cause me to be derailed. I didn't let the flaws that people imposed on me publicly hurt my spirit.

So if you take anything away from this point of inspiration I feel I am creating for you, it is to remember who you are. Silence the noise, focus, and research. These things will enable you to have a great outlook on where you are headed as you go through the daily battles in your immediate life. Good luck, ladies!

MEET THE
VISIONARY AUTHOR

LILA HOLLEY

Lila Holley is a retired US Army Chief Warrant Officer Four and award-winning, Amazon #1 bestselling author of three books. In her book, *Battle Buddy: Maneuvering the Battlefield of Transitioning from the Military,* Lila chronicles how she battled issues with depression and anger during her transition in order to help military members and Veterans through the emotional process of transitioning from military life to civilian life.

Lila is the visionary author behind *Camouflaged Sisters: Revealing Struggles of the Black Woman's Military Experience* and *Camouflaged Sisters: Silent No More,* through which she partnered with other courageous female service members and women Veterans to share their stories of success in the military despite facing challenges along their journey. She's created multiple media platforms—in radio, magazines, and online—where military women connect with each other, gain resources, and share their stories.

Contact Lila at csinfo@camouflagedsisters.com or at her website www.camouflagedsisters.com

MEET THE COAUTHORS

Duty to Family

ABENI CELESTE SCOTT

Abeni Celeste Scott was born in Miami, Florida, and joined the Army in February 1997, serving as a 92A, automated logistics specialists. In 2010, she transitioned to the rank of Warrant Officer. An expert in her field, Abeni retired in March 2017 with twenty years of service. She is currently pursuing her master's degree in professional counseling at Grand Canyon University. In September 2016, she launched a fashion boutique for women called Dress Up Room By Four Girls.

ANGEL RHODES

Angel is currently serving in the US Army. She is married to her high school sweetheart, Brent, and they have three beautiful children, Bre-Jon, Breanna, and Xavier. In addition to serving her country, Angel is cofounder and CEO of Marriage of God, LLC, where she and Brent work together as certified marriage and relationship builders. They use biblical principles to help clients create actionable strategies to improve their relationships and marriages.

Learn more at marriageofgod.com

DE'MEATRICE 'DEE DEE' HODGES

After graduating high school, Dee Dee Hodges enlisted in the US Army. While serving on one of her many deployments in support of Operation Iraqi Freedom, she was wounded in action, earning the coveted Purple Heart Medal. Dee Dee medically retired in June 2009 due to health reasons, and now, she sings around the world. Her first album is due out summer of 2017. She resides in Killeen, Texas, with her husband, Michael, and daughter, Jelecia.

Learn more at deedeehodges.com

FANNY MINNITT

Fanny Minnitt is a radio host, author, Veteran, and retired educator who now serves as a licensed minister committed to sharing the message of faith and drawing people back to God's Word. Fanny recently traveled to Nairobi, Kenya, to share the message of faith at Jesus Healing Sanctuary Ministries International Power Conference. She holds a master's degree in education from Tarleton State University and is a former contributing writer for the *Anchor Newspaper* in Waco, Texas.

Learn more at fannyminnitt.com

FATIMA R. WILLIAMS

Fatima R. Williams is a US Air Force Veteran who honorably served for nine years. Fatima grew up an "Army brat" and understands the sacrifices made by service members and their families. Fatima, along with her husband Army Veteran Bryn Williams and their two adult daughters, reside in Texas. Fatima now serves as an entrepreneur in the financial industry with a goal to empower women to live life financially free! God, family, and service!

For more information, visit Myfes.net/fwilliams6

SHANNON CLARK

Shannon D. Clark is an Army Veteran, proud wife, and mother from Newport News, Virginia. She is currently serving in Dahlonega, Georgia, as a military science instructor. As a Soldier and wellness coach, Shannon lives to enrich the lives of others. Through her expertise in resilience coaching, health education, and stress reduction, her goal is to inspire people to reach their full potential mentally, physically, and spiritually.

Learn more by emailing her at
instructorsclark@gmail.com

SHARON FINNEY

Sharon Finney is an Army Veteran who uses writing as a method of dealing with life challenges, such as deployment, separation, and death. While recognizing how words can heal and encourage, she has written previously for *DIGEST THIS! Ministry Magazine.* Sharon is a devoted wife and mother who also enjoys charitable endeavors. She has a bachelor of science in music and a master of arts in human services.

Sharon Finney can be contacted at
authorsharonfinney@gmail.com

TAMARA PURNELL

Tamara Purnell lives in Baltimore, Maryland. She is a Navy Veteran, retired Baltimore City sheriff, minister, and community servant. In 2016, Tamara ran for the 7th District City Council seat, the home of Freddie Gray, the African American man who died in police custody. She worked to bring calm to the district during riots that ensued following Gray's death. Tamara is the proud mother of one daughter and grandmother of three. Her motto is, "Be the best you that you can be."

TAREKA ROBINSON

Tareka Robinson was born and raised in Cleveland, Mississippi. She graduated from East Side High School in 2000 and then attended Jackson State University where she earned a bachelor of administration in management. While at Jackson State University, Tareka became a member of Delta Sigma Theta Sorority. She currently resides in Nashville, Tennessee, and is the founder and operator of Virtuous Hats, a public relations business she started in April 2016.

Contact Tareka at email tarekarobinson@gmail.com
or virtuoushatspr@gmail.com

Duty to Serve

ASHLEY M. BOOKER

Ashley M. Booker is a Veteran of the US Army with over ten years of honorable service. She created a movement, I Stand for Positivity, to help people in Central Texas focus on positivity daily and what's really important in life: love. Ashley is the mother of two amazing children and serves as an influential parental figure for dozens of children through her daycare in Central Texas. Ashley's motto for life is "Lead from the front."

DR. KAREN MAXFIELD-LUNKIN

Dr. Karen Maxfield-Lunkin is a US Army Veteran and an entrepreneur with close to twenty-five years of experience as a teacher, mentor, administrator, parent coach, educational advocate, and pastor. Described as a thought leader and innovator, Dr. Karen speaks, leads workshops, and coaches workshops that lead to creative collaboration. She created the BridgeUcation Creative Consulting Group where she serves as a book writing coach, inspiring future authors to write the books inside of them. *Imagine the unimaginable, then create it!*

KRISTINA EATON

Kristina Eaton is a certified life coach, a US Army Logistics Officer, speaker, and advocate for literacy. She is also the founder and CEO of Formation Coaching Group, LLC, a life-coaching firm that helps women with emotional healing and finding life fulfillment. Kristina is a bestselling coauthor of three anthologies: *W.O.M.B. Sisters Chronicles Vol 1, Delayed But Not Denied: 20 Inspirational Stories About Life and Resiliency,* and *20 Beautiful Women Vol 4.*

Learn more at www.iamkristinae.com

MICHELE M. SPENCER

Michele M. Spencer is an Army Reserve Medical Service Corps Lieutenant Colonel assigned to the Office of the Surgeon General's Patient Care Integration in Virginia. She has been serving her country for over thirty years. Michele is an Operation Iraqi Freedom Veteran, a registered yoga teacher, and Reiki master. She holds a master's degree in exercise science and is the author of *B.A.G.H.D.A.D. Yoga A Shift in Consciousness: Fear to Love, War to Peace.*

Learn more at www.michelespencer.com

MICHELE PATTON JOHNSON

Michele Patton Johnson's mission is to see people set free and walking in wholeness. Her passion is to enlighten women about who God created them to be. Michele is a certified life coach, human behavior consultant, and certified image consultant, and she is the founder of In Our Image Coaching and Consulting. Married and mother to two adult children, Michele is still serving in the Army and looking forward to retirement.

Learn more at www.inourimage126.com

NIKEISHA JOHNSON

Nikeisha Johnson is a Captain in the US Army, wife of CW3 Anthony Johnson, mother, college professor, minister, motivational speaker, and current doctoral student. She has a BS in psychology, an MA in health psychology, and an MS in clinical psychology. Nikeisha's passion is to encourage, empower, and restore all who have been broken, wounded, and torn. Her desire is to help others embrace the uniqueness that God placed within them.

For more information, email
embraceyouruniqueness@yahoo.com

PATRICIA LAW

Patricia Law is a retired US Army Veteran who served honorably for twenty-one years, with a deployment in support of Desert Storm. She was the last class of the Women's Army Corps (WAC) in 1978. She holds an associate's degree in criminal justice and works with the Bell County Juvenile Justice Alternative Education Program. She loves helping and motivating others to not give up and trust God. Patricia is married with two children and has five granddaughters.

RADIAH MALLARD

Radiah Mallard is a proud Veteran with twenty-one years of service in the US Army and Navy. As a senior Warrant Officer, Radiah served two tours in Iraq, gained extensive experience in her career field in a combat zone, and received recognition by the Department of the Army. She is a mother of four children and an advocate for her level three autistic son, who is nonverbal. Radiah and her husband are owners of multiple businesses.

Duty to Self

ADENA TUFTS

Adena Tufts is originally from Cleveland, Ohio. Knowing that her divine purpose was to become a nurse, Adena currently works as a critical care nurse, which allows her to walk in her gift of loving and encouraging others back to life both physically and spiritually. She is currently a travel nurse administering care to children in a pediatric intensive care unit.

CATHY A. GRANT

Cathy A. Grant is a retired US Army Sergeant First Class (E-7) from Chicago, Illinois. She is the sixth child of Catherine Cartlidge and Ollie Cartlidge (deceased). Cathy currently resides in Texas with her husband, Dale, daughter, Sherise, and stepdaughter, Skylar. Following her twenty-one year career, Cathy now serves women as an entrepreneur with Mary Kay where she gives back to domestic violence survivors.

Contact her at Ladyc_66442@yahoo.com

CSILLA TOTH

Csilla Toth is a blogger who writes about Christian values, family, and parenting. She is passionate about teaching and music. She and her husband have been married for twenty-two years and have five amazing children. She holds a bachelor's degree in primary school teaching specializing in music education. Csilla is a Sergeant in the US Army and actively participates in her unit's mentorship program called Sisters in Arms.

Learn more at www.csillatothblog.wordpress.com

DANNIELLE RAMOS RASH

Dannielle Ramos Rash of First Class Résumés & Career Services provides federal résumés and career documents for job seekers, specializing in helping transitioning military members. Dannielle's been featured in *Mastering Your Career Journey: 11 Career Experts Share the Secrets to Success*, *Modernize Your Job Search Letters: Get Noticed...Get Hired*, and *Forward March Magazine*, a biannual magazine released in May and November.

Learn more at www.first-classresumes.com and allow her to Take You Higher to get Hired!™

DIANE MOSLEY

Diane is a friend, a confidant, and an international speaker who teaches and speaks to professional groups and church groups. Diane has always had a passion for helping others. A former Sunday school teacher and believer of the Word of God, she mentors children and adults. Diane currently works as an executive with the federal government.

DONNA RAMIREZ

Donna Ramirez is married with three children and two grandchildren. During her military career, Donna served as a cook and earned multiple awards. She resides in Killeen, Texas, and owns a home-based business named Gifts and Creations. She enjoys helping others and continues to serve her community by volunteering at the local soup kitchen, nursing home, her church Agape C.O.G.I.C., and a local nonprofit organization called Helping the Hands that Feed the Homeless.

EBONY JOHNSON

Ebony Johnson is a US Air Force Veteran. She is founder and president of The Next Chapter Corporation, a nonprofit that provides services to Veterans and survivors of sexual assault and domestic violence. Ebony is also founder and CEO of Success Creators, which provides executive career coaching and resume writing services. Ebony was the recipient of the 2016 Dunkin' Donuts Community Hero Award and the 2015 Next Generation of Government Innovator of the Year Award.

Learn more at www.simplyebony.com

KALEN ARREOLA

Kalen Arreola is the president and founder of Kalen Marie Consulting. She was a Captain in the US Army Reserve serving as a public affairs officer for ten years in Nashville, Tennessee; Denver, Colorado; and Southern California. During the surge, Kalen deployed to Iraq, where she was awarded the Bronze Star Medal for leadership. Since 2009, Kalen has run a successful marketing consulting firm and the nonprofit Pinups for Patriots.

Learn more at kalenmarieconsulting.com and pinupsforpatriots.com

SOPHIA L. ELLIS

Sophia L. Ellis was born in Aiken, South Carolina, and raised in New York and Atlanta. She has actively served in the Army Reserves since 2002. Sophia has a bachelor's degree in business administration and a master's degree in project management. She is the author of the children's books *Tre: The Extraordinaire* and *Through the Eyes of Tre*. Sophia founded Youth with Ambition, LLC, to teach youth to discover and develop their natural skills and talent.

Learn more at www.sophialellis.com/

DR. TAMARA P. WILLIAMS

Dr. Tamara P. Williams is the founder of Aramat & Associates, Inc., an author, educator, public speaker, and Veteran of the US Air Force. Dr. Williams's expertise is in business, leadership, and federal acquisitions and various aspects of government contracting. Aramat & Associates, Inc., helps customers strategize on ways to obtain government business. This information is also disseminated through the weekly Internet show *Business 101 with Dr. Tamara Williams* at www.radiovps.com.

TAWANDA HARRIS

Tawanda Harris is a retired US Army Major. She was a distinguished military graduate from Lincoln University, Missouri, where she earned a bachelor's degree in liberal studies. Tawanda also has a master's degree in environmental management from Webster University and a certification in homeland security. Her highest military awards include three Meritorious Service Medals and one Bronze Star Medal. She resides in Vine Grove, Kentucky, with her devoted husband, Deven.

Contact Tawanda at tawanharris@gmail.com

TC JORDAN

TC Jordan is a retired, disabled Veteran of the US Air Force and a level 3 nationally certified sexual assault victim advocate of thirteen years. She is also the proud founder and owner of Xokiahi Cares, Inc., an unconventional nonprofit that seeks out the needs of the community in order to find viable solutions. She currently resides on the island of Guam, where she attends the University of Guam to pursue a master's degree in counseling.

1. TAKE A PHOTO

Take a pic of you with a Camouflaged Sisters book.

2. CAPTION IT

Tell us what you thought of the book.

3. TAG IT

Tag us @CamouflagedSisters and Hashtag it up #BehindtheRank #SilentNoMore and of course

#CamouflagedSisters

Visit us at
camouflagedsisters.com

**purposely
created**
P U B L I S H I N G

CREATING DISTINCTIVE BOOKS
WITH INTENTIONAL RESULTS

We're a collaborative group of creative masterminds
with a mission to produce high-quality books to position
you for monumental success in the marketplace.

Our professional team of writers, editors, designers,
and marketing strategists work closely together to ensure
that every detail of your book is a clear representation
of the message in your writing.

Want to know more?
Write to us at info@publishyourgift.com
or call (888) 949-6228

Discover great books, exclusive offers, and more at
www.PublishYourGift.com

Connect with us on social media

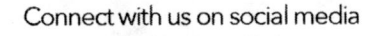

@publishyourgift